The Layman's Guide To Counseling

by Susan J. Wallace

PNEUMA LIFE
PUBLISHING

The Layman's Guide to Counseling

by Susan J. Wallace

Published by: **PNEUMA LIFE**
PUBLISHING

All Scripture quotations, unless noted otherwise, are from the Holy Bible.

All rights reserved. No part of this book may be reproduced in any form without permission in writing from the publisher, except in the case of brief quotations embodied in church related publications, critical articles or reviews.

Quotations from the King James Version have been denoted (KJV). All emphasis within quotations is the author's addition.

Printed in the United States of America

Copyright © 1993 -Susan J. Wallace

The Layman's Guide to Counseling
ISBN 1-56229-408-3

Pneuma Life Publishing
P.O. Box 10612
Bakersfield, CA 93389
(805) 324-1741

Table of Contents

ACKNOWLEDGEMENTS

INTRODUCTION

LESSON 1. BASIC PRINCIPLES OF WORD-BASED COUNSELING   11
      Definition of word-based counseling
      The process of counseling
      Steps in counseling

LESSON 2. SALVATION AND ASSURANCE   21
      The necessity for the new birth
      From death to life
      The results of the new birth
      Redemption and the counselor

LESSON 3. BAPTISM IN THE HOLY SPIRIT   33
      Who the Holy Spirit is
      The ministry of the Holy Spirit
      Baptism in the Holy Spirit

LESSON 4. MARRIAGE AND FAMILY COUNSELING   47
      Definition of marriage and family counseling
      Marital relations
      Parent/child relationship

LESSON 5. YOUTH COUNSELING   61
      Understanding children and youth
      Physical & emotional characteristics,
         interests and needs
      Counseling techniques

LESSON 6. CRISIS COUNSELING   77
      Definition of crisis counseling
      Counseling those in crisis
      A crisis counseling format

LESSON 7. PHYSICAL HEALING   89
    The gifts of healing
    The causes of illness
    Why we are sent to heal the sick
    God's provision for the manifestation
        of His healing power
    Some things that block healing
    Equipping the counselor for ministry
    Some healing do's and don'ts

LESSON 8. INNER HEALING   103
    Definition of inner healing
    How memories get healed
    Ministering inner healing
    Methods of inner healing
    Inner healing prayers
    The importance of forgiveness in inner healing
    Qualifications of the counselor for inner healing

LESSON 9. ABUSE   115
    Understanding abuse
    Some types of abusers
    Counseling the abuser
    Counseling the abused

LESSON 10. DEMON DELIVERANCE   125
    Definition of deliverance
    Spiritual bondage
    The importance of deliverance
    Determining the need for deliverance
    Demon manifestation
    Casting out demons
    Preventing the return of demons
    Self deliverance
    A counselor as a deliverance minister

Charts / Tables / Lists

1. **ABUSE**
   Counseling Approaches 12
   The Basic Skills 14
   Human Difficulties 16
   Summary of Counseling Steps 18

2. **SALVATION AND ASSURANCE**
   Necessity For the New Birth 22
   From Death to Life 1 23
   From Death to Life 2 25
   The Reconciling Work of Christ 27
   Ministering Salvation 29

3. **BAPTISM IN THE HOLY SPIRIT**
   Who Is the Holy Spirit? 33
   The Ministry of the Holy Spirit 35
   What Baptism In the Holy Spirit Means 38
   Speaking In Tongues 39
   Ministering the Baptism In the Holy Spirit 42

4. **MARRIAGE AND FAMILY COUNSELING**
   Components of A Good Marriage 47
   Anticipating Marriage 49
   One Saved Spouse 51
   Saved Wife and Unsaved Husband 52
   Contemplating Divorce 1 53
   Contemplating Divorce 2 54
   Parent / Child Relationship 56

5. **YOUTH COUNSELING**
   Behavior Characteristics: Age 6 - 9 years 64
   Behavior Characteristics: Age 10 - 13 years 65
   Behavior Characteristics: Teenagers 66
   Symptomatic Behavior 69

6. CRISIS COUNSELING
    The Elements of Crisis 77
    Analysis of Crisis Situation 81
    Inventory of the Individual 83
    Direction In Response to Issues 85
    A Crisis Counseling Format 87

7. PHYSICAL HEALING
    Causes of Sickness 90
    Motives For Healing 93
    Avenues and Methods For Healing 95
    Healing Blocks 98
    Equipping the Counselor 100
    Helpful Hints For Healing 102

8. INNER HEALING
    What Is Inner Healing? 104
    How Memories Are Stored In the Soul 105
    Detecting the Need For Inner Healing 108
    Requirements For the Counselor 112
    Characteristics of A Counselor 113

9. ABUSE
    Types of Abuse 115
    Counseling the Abuser 119
    Counseling the Abused 121

10. DEMON DELIVERANCE
    What Is Deliverance? 125
    How Demons Enter 128
    Why Deliverance? 130
    Determining the Need For Deliverance 131
    Preventing the Return of Demons 138

ACKNOWLEDGMENTS

I owe untold gratitude to God Almighty for providing me with His Word which I have found to be a most effective agent of physical, psychological and spiritual healing.

Thanks to my husband, Sydney, for his love, support and understanding, and to my Pastor, the Rev. Dr. E. Etienne E. Bowleg for affording me the opportunity to teach this course as a pioneer program.

I am also most grateful to a number of people who have inspired me in the writing of this book, and whose works have been a source of information and confirmation for me. Among them are Dennis and Rita Bennett, Clyde M. Narramore, Reuel Howe, Selwyn Hughes, Professor Paul Welter, Grunlan Lambrides, James Kennedy, Norman H. Wright, Frank and Ida Mae Hammond, Winn Worley, Charles and Frances Hunter, Billy Graham, and Pat Robertson.

DEDICATION

To Joanna Alexandria Bethel,
my mother and spiritual friend

INTRODUCTION

The increasing work of the Pastor in counseling his parishioners, is making him more and more aware of the need to raise up lay-counselors to share this burden with him. The objectives of this book are, therefore, as follows:

1. To serve as an education in word-based counseling for the layman counselor himself.
2. To provide an opportunity for whatever healing he requires in any of the areas dealt with.
3. To serve as a manual for the layman instructor in word-based counseling.
4. To be used as a text book by the student pursuing this course in word-based counseling.

The course is designed to be a ten week or ten session program with a practical exercise at the end of each session. It is also intended that each lesson taught, would be the basis for real practice during the interim period between lessons.

A number of visual aids in the form of charts, lists, and tables, is an attempt to make the program as simple and effective as possible. Each session deals with a different area of Counseling, covering topics as seen in the Table of Contents.

LESSON 1

BASIC PRINCIPLES OF WORD-BASED COUNSELING

I. DEFINITION OF WORD-BASED COUNSELING

A. Definition

1. The word "counsel" is derived from the Hebrew word "ya'ats" meaning: advice in the form of guidance and direction.

2. Word-based counseling is a ministry dealing with the whole person - spirit, soul, and body.

3. It does not look to man for healing, but is totally dependent upon the Word of God to discover the root causes of the counselee's problem.

4. It looks to Jesus, through the power of the Holy Spirit, to set the counselee free from spiritual, emotional, and physical bondage (Ps.107:20).

B. What the Scriptures Say About Counseling

1. Old Testament

    (a) Wisdom is found in those who take advice (Prov.13:10).

    (b) David talks about the "sweet" counsel of a friend (Ps. 55:13,14).

(c) Jethro gave advice to his son-in-law, Moses, to share his responsibilities with able men who fear the Lord (Ex. 18:5-26).

(d) Rehoboam, son of Solomon, sought counsel of the elders who served Solomon, on how to answer those who sought relief from taxes. He did not, however, act on their counsel (1 Kings 12:9,28).

2. New Testament

(a) Five approaches to counseling as outlined in Grunlan Lambrides' book, "Healing Relationships":
"Now we exhort you brethren, warn those who are unruly, comfort the faint-hearted, uphold the weak, be patient with all" (1 Thess. 5:14).

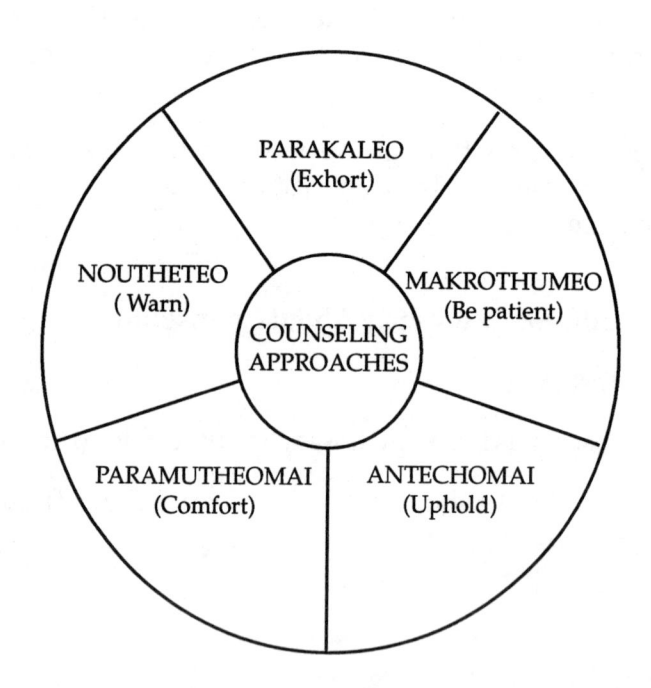

```
                    PARAKALEO
                     (Exhort)

  NOUTHETEO                      MAKROTHUMEO
   (Warn)                         (Be patient)
              COUNSELING
              APPROACHES

  PARAMUTHEOMAI                  ANTECHOMAI
    (Comfort)                     (Uphold)
```

C. The Difference Between Christian and Secular Counseling

1. Christian Counseling

    (a) It is directive and encourages the use of the Bible.

    (b) It seeks to bring the principles of God's Word to bear on human problems, telling people with deep compassion and genuine love, what God requires of them.

2. Secular Counseling

    (a) It is non-directive.

    (b) It encourages one to look within himself for solutions.

D. Who Is Called to Counsel?

1. All Christians are called to minister to each other.

    (a) "Let each of you look out not only for his own interests, but also for the interests of others" (Phil. 2:4).

    (b) "Bear one another's burdens and so fulfill the law of Christ" (Gal. 6:2).

    (c) "Therefore comfort each other and edify one another, just as you also are doing" (1 Thess. 5:11).

2. All Christians are called to minister to each other and they do, but do they counsel effectively?

    e.g.   - parent/child counseling

    - neighbor/neighbor counseling

    - teacher/student counseling

Our relationship with the Lord should affect our relationship with one another. Some people are supernaturally gifted and should pursue counseling further.

II. THE PROCESS OF COUNSELING

A professional counselor has to learn numerous techniques and principles to enable him to effectively help people through their problems. Selwyn Hughes in his book, "Helping People Through Their Problems," feels that as lay counselors, we can reduce these techniques to ten basic skills, understanding them, practicing them, and relying on the Holy Spirit's help to make us more effective in another person's life.

Basic Principles of Word-Based Counseling

THE BASIC SKILLS

1. Be a good listener.
2. Evaluate the person's level of need.
3. Accept people as they are.
4. Empathize with hurt feelings.
5. Be careful what you say and how you say it.
6. Distinguish between causes and symptoms.
7. Keep confidences.
8. Use questions wisely.
9. Watch your body language.
10. Don't be drawn in out of your depth.

A. The Basic Skills

1. Be a good listener
"Therefore, my beloved brethren, let every man be swift to hear, slow to speak, slow to wrath..." (James 1:19)

- (a) Norman H. Wright's definition of listening: "Listening is not thinking about what we are going to say when the other person has stopped talking." In doing this, we tune people out, and sometimes miss vital information.

- (b) Counselors should be trained in the art of listening. Listening does not come naturally; it must be developed. It was said that the reason God gave us two ears and only one mouth, is so that we can do twice as much listening as talking.

- (c) People have a great need to be listened to. Sometimes all they need is an attentive ear.

- (d) Hear the other person's feelings and reasons; pay attention to gestures, mannerisms, and tone of voice.

- (e) Treat the counselee as you would wish to be treated. Avoid nagging and criticizing.

2. Evaluate the person's level of need, recognizing that the level of need determines the urgency with which assistance must be given and the manner in which you proceed.
Professor Paul Welter defines five areas of human difficulties. Most issues are in the area of problems and predicaments.

- (a) Areas of difficulties
    - (i) The problem - has a solution.
    - (ii) The predicament - has no easy solution.
    - (iii) The crisis - needs immediate, urgent action.

    (iv) Panic - the person is disoriented and irrational.
    (v) Shock - the mind lapses for minutes or hours.

HUMAN DIFFICULTIES

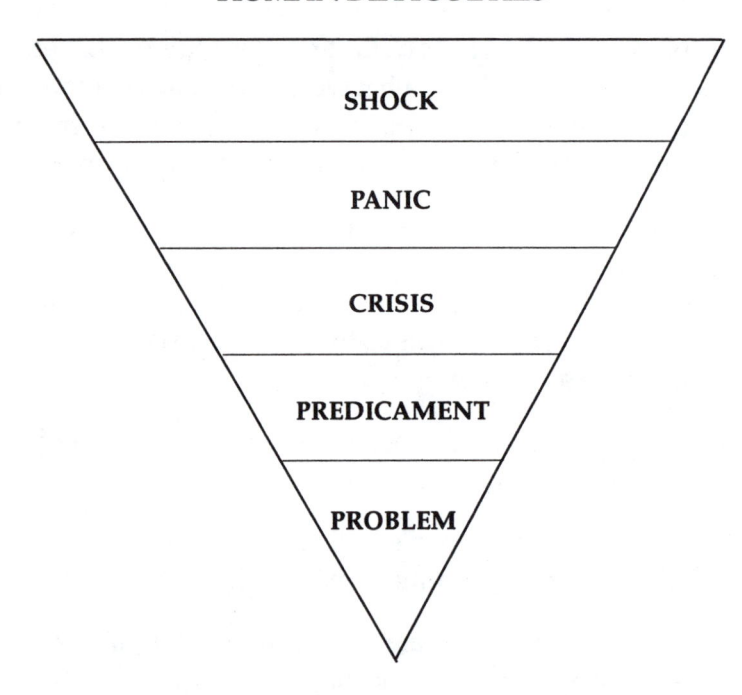

```
         SHOCK
         PANIC
         CRISIS
       PREDICAMENT
         PROBLEM
```

3. Accept people as they are.

    (a) Adopt a non-judgmental attitude and develop a relationship with the person.

    (b) God does the changing from inside.

    (c) It is the grace of God that makes the difference.

4. Empathize with hurt feelings

Greek: "sumpathees" - not feeling sorry for, but feeling the same thing as the other.

Basic Principles Of Word-Based Counseling 17

  (a) Identify with the person's feelings. See things from the other's perspective.

  (b) Jesus empathized: "For we do not have a high priest who is unable to sympathize with our weakness..."

5. **Be careful what you say and how you say it.**

  (a) Reflect a genuine interest and concern *(Prov. 27:9)*.

  (b) Pause. It will convey in non-verbal language, your own personal grief and concern.

  (c) Do not give advice. Help the person think the issues through.

  (d) Repeat to the person a summary of the problem as you see it, eliminating the problem of misconception.

  (e) Add a few questions and discuss a few Bible verses with relation to the problem.

6. **Distinguish between causes and symptoms.**

  (a) The cause is the root of the problem.

  (b) The symptom may be eliminated for a time but returns if the cause is not eliminated.

7. **Keep confidence.**

  (a) If you cannot keep a confidence when someone shares with you, you should not be on the counseling team.

  (b) A Christian counselor has this responsibility.

8. **Use questions wisely.**

  (a) Don't ask too many questions, and avoid a series of questions, as these could be threatening.

(b) Avoid either/or questions, and ask "why" sparingly.

(c) Ask open-ended questions: e.g. What are some of the ways your parents have influenced you?

9. **Watch your body language**.

    (a) Be careful with your facial expressions, body posture, and general appearance. Look into the counselee's eyes. Fifty percent of our expressions are facial expressions.

    (b) Look at people when you minister to them.

10. **Do not be drawn in out of your depth**.

    (a) Refer the counselee when you are not equipped to handle the problem.

    (b) Refer to a minister.

III. STEPS IN COUNSELING

Step I	Listen attentively to what the counselee has to say
Step II	Allow the Holy Spirit to identify for you the areas to be healed.
Step III	Deal with these areas one by one.
Step IV	Counsel with the rhema Word of God given to you by the Holy Spirit.
Step V	Encourage counselee to share his reactions.
Step VI	Pray with the counselee for healing or other needs as necessary.

Step VII   Refer counselee to Pastor or professional counselor if required.

Step VIII Insist on counselee implementing the advice given and arrange for further counseling if necessary.

A. Listen Attentively to What the Counselee Has to Say

Sometimes, all the counselee needs is a listening ear.

B. Allow the Holy Spirit to Identify For You the Areas to be Healed

Pray either silently or with the counselee, sharing verbal praise and thanksgiving. The Holy Spirit will bring to your memory what you need to do or say.

C. Deal With These Areas One By One

It is less painful. Breaking one stick at a time is easier than trying to break a whole bundle together.

D. Counsel With the Rhema Word of God Given to You By the Holy Spirit

The Word of God is living and powerful and sharper than any two edged sword... *(Heb. 4:12)*. God's word never fails *(1 Kings 8:56)*.

E. Encourage Counselee To Share His Reactions

It is important to know what he feels, for sometimes his feelings or emotions may also need healing.

F. Pray With the Counselee For Healing or Other Needs As Necessary

Pray with him for salvation if he is not a born-again Christian. Assure the counselee that God hears the prayers of His believers when they claim His promises in the name of Jesus *(John 14:13,14)*.

G. Refer the Counselee to A Pastor or Professional Counselor If Required

The counselor should recognize when he is out of his depth.

H. Insist On Counselee Implementing the Advice Given and Arrange For Further Counseling If Necessary

Theory must be translated into practice. Faith without works is dead *(James 2:26b)*.

IV. PRACTICAL

A. Form teams of two to enact a typical counseling session using the techniques used above. Let participants volunteer situations involving either themselves or others they know.

B. On returning to the class let the counselee give an objective criticism of the counselor according to the guidelines given in the lesson.

LESSON 2

SALVATION AND ASSURANCE

I. THE NECESSITY FOR THE NEW BIRTH

Rita and Dennis Bennett in their book, "Trinity Of Man", show an interesting diagram on the relationship between the spirit, soul, and body of man. The chart overpage, based on the same concept, compares the state of man before and after the new birth. Discuss the trinity of man from this chart.

A. Qualifications For Admission to the Kingdom of Heaven

1. The new birth.

    (a) Nicodemus was told by Jesus that unless he was born again, he could not enter into the kingdom of heaven (*John 3:3,5*).

B. Our Dead Spirits Must Be Regenerated

1. "That which is born of the flesh is flesh and that which is born of the Spirit is spirit" (*John 3:6*).

C. We Must Be Made Alive to God

1. "And you He made alive, who were dead in trespasses and sins, in which you once walked according to the course of this world, according to the prince of the power of the air, the spirit who now works in the sons of disobedience" (*Eph. 2:1,2*).

We see from the chart, man's condition before and after the new birth has taken place. We see the being of man in its unregenerate state with its senses attuned to the world, its spirit dead and its soul in control. After salvation, he is transformed to a spirit alive in Christ, restoring fellowship with God and enabling the spirit's control of the being of man.

NECESSITY FOR THE NEW BIRTH

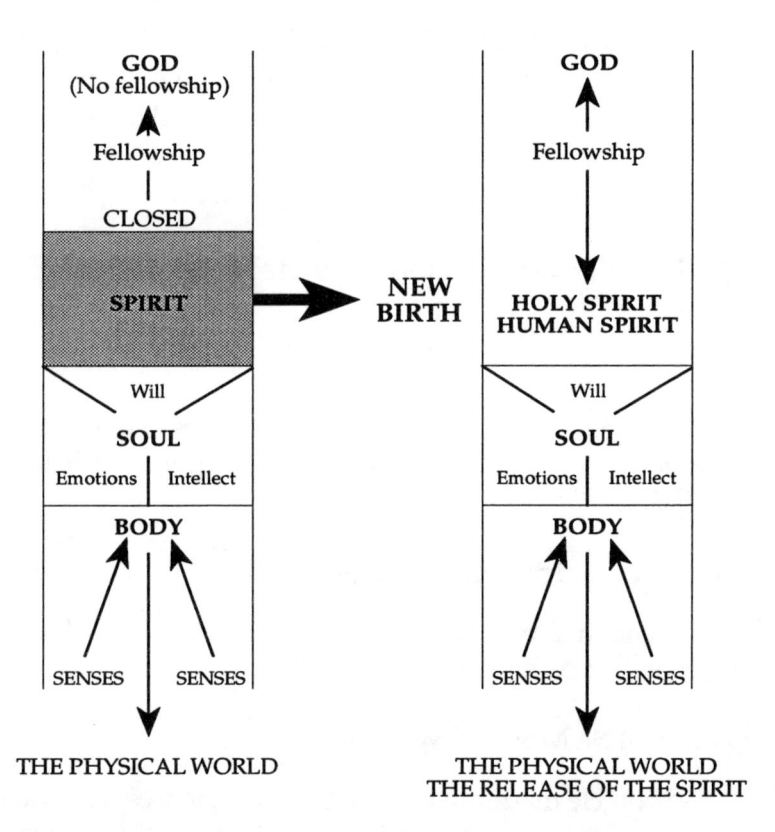

```
        GOD                                    GOD
  (No fellowship)                               ▲
        ▲                                       |
    Fellowship                              Fellowship
        |                                       ▼
     CLOSED
                          NEW
     SPIRIT        →     BIRTH          HOLY SPIRIT
                                        HUMAN SPIRIT

        Will                                   Will
       SOUL                                   SOUL
  Emotions | Intellect                  Emotions | Intellect
       BODY                                   BODY
        ▲   ▲                                  ▲   ▲
   SENSES  SENSES                         SENSES  SENSES
        ▼                                       ▼
  THE PHYSICAL WORLD                    THE PHYSICAL WORLD
                                       THE RELEASE OF THE SPIRIT
```

Qualifications for admission to the kingdom of heaven (John 3:3,5)

Our spirits must be regenerated (John 3:6)

We must be made alive to God (Eph. 2:1)

II. FROM DEATH TO LIFE

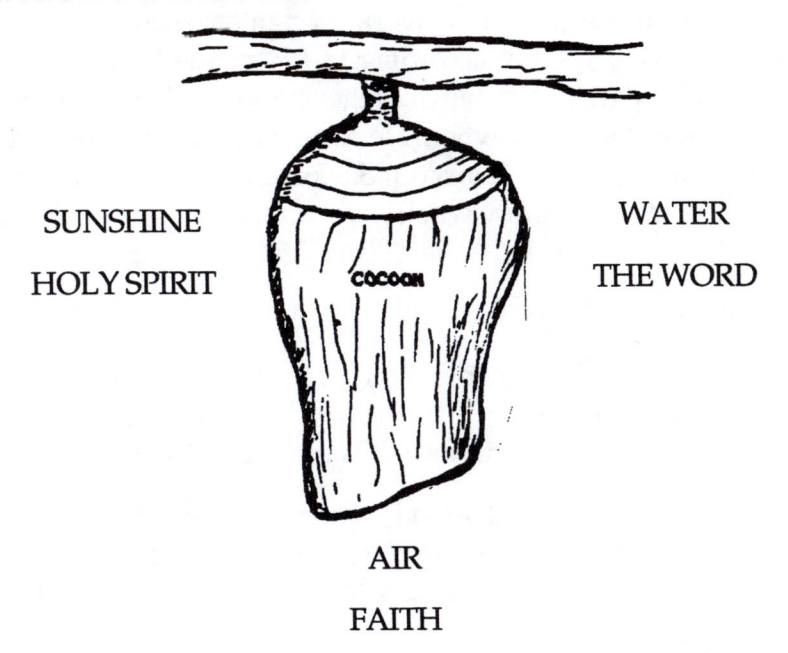

SUNSHINE
HOLY SPIRIT

COCOON

WATER
THE WORD

AIR

FAITH

Renewing by the Holy Spirit (Titus 3:5-7)

Born-again through the word of God (1 Peter 1:23)

Born of God through belief and faith in Christ (1 John 5:1)

A. How The New Birth Is Produced

1. By the Holy Spirit

   (a) Being born of the Holy Spirit: Jesus answered, "Most assuredly, I say to you, unless one is born of water and the Spirit, he cannot enter into the kingdom of God" (John 3:5)

(b) Through washing, regeneration and renewing of the Holy Spirit. "not by works of righteousness which we have done, but according to His mercy He saved us, through the washing of regeneration and renewing of the Holy Spirit, whom He poured out on us abundantly through Jesus Christ our Savior, that having been justified by His grace we should become heirs according to the hope of eternal life" *(Titus 3:5-7)*.

2. By the word of God

    (a) Brought forth by the Word of truth. "Of His own will, He brought us forth by the word of truth, that we might be a kind of firstfruits of His creatures" *(James 1:18)*.

    (b) Born of the word of God. "Having been born again, not of corruptible seed but incorruptible, through the word of God which lives and abides forever..." (1 Pet.1:23).

3. By faith.

    (a) Belief that Jesus is the Christ. "Whoever believes that Jesus is the Christ is born of God, and everyone who loves Him who begot, also loves Him who is begotten of Him" (1 John 5:1).

    (b) Belief in the resurrection of Jesus Christ.

    "if you confess with your mouth the Lord Jesus and believe in your heart that God has raised Him from the dead, you will be saved. For with the heart one believes to righteousness, and with the mouth confession is made to salvation" (Rom.10:9,10).

III. THE RESULTS OF THE NEW BIRTH

BUTTERFLY	CHRISTIAN
1. Airborne	Spirit regenerated (Eph. 2:4,5)
2. Transformation	A new creation (2 Cor. 5:17)
3. Mobility	Assurance of Salvation (John 10:28,29)
4. Purpose	Love for God (Deut. 30:6)
5. Pollination	Love for one another (1 John 3:10)
6. Constancy	Holy Life (1 John 3:9)
7. Fulfillment of purpose	Victorious living (1 John 5:4,5)

A. The New Creature

1. Anyone in Christ. "therefore if anyone is in Christ, he is a new creation; old things have passed away; behold all things have become new" *(2 Cor. 5:17)*.

B. Changed Life

1. Circumcision of the heart. God spoke to Israel and told them that if they would obey His voice: "the Lord your God will circumcise your heart and the heart of your descendants, to love the Lord your God with all your heart and with all your soul, that you may live" *(Deut. 30:6)*.

   (a) Requires obedience to God.

   (b) Requires loving God.

2. Living a holy life. "Whoever has been born of God does not sin, for His seed remains in him; and he cannot sin, because he has been born of God" *(1 John 3:9)*.

3. Loving one another. "whoever does not practice righteousness is not of God, nor is he who does not love his brother" *(1 John 3:10)*.

C. Victorious Living

1. Whoever is born of God is an overcomer. "For whatever is born of God overcomes the world. And this is the victory that has overcome the world - our faith. Who is he who overcomes the world, but he who believes that Jesus is the Son of God" *(1 John 5:4,5)*

   (a) Faith overcomes the world.

   (b) The old man was crucified with Christ.

   (c) We must also rise with Him.

D. Assurance Of Eternal Life

1. Jesus assures us of eternal life. "And I give them eternal life, and they shall never perish; neither shall anyone snatch

them out of My hand. My Father, who has given them to Me, is greater than all; and no one is able to snatch them out of My Father's hand" *(John 10:28,29)*.

(a) No one is able to snatch us out of the Father's hand, but we have free will to remove ourselves from His hand.

IV. REDEMPTION AND THE COUNSELOR

RECONCILING WORK OF CHRIST

1. The Need for Love (1 John 4:7,8)
   God Is the Source of Love

2. Acceptance (Romans 5:6,7)
   Christ Died For the Ungodly

3. Discipline (Deut. 30:19)
   A Choice Between Life and Death

A. The Reconciling Work of Christ

Reuel Howe in his book, "Man's Need And God's Action" (1952) suggests three basic needs that are met through the reconciling work of God in Christ. These are especially important to Christian counselors:

1. The need for love

   (a) God is the true source of love. "Beloved, let us love one another for love is of God; and everyone who loves is born of God and knows God. He who does not love does not know God, for God is love" *(1 John 4:7,8)*.

(b) Because we have been loved and forgiven by God, we are able to accept the weaknesses and failings of those we counsel.

2. Acceptance

(a) God accepts us as we are. "For when we were still without strength, in due time Christ died for the ungodly. For scarcely for a righteous man will one die..." *(Rom. 5:6,7a)*.

(b) Because God accepts us, we can accept our counselees as they are.

3. Discipline

(a) Discipline is not rules and punishment, but boundaries for our protection and guidance.

(b) It is the source of true human freedom. Freedom involves choice: the choice between God and Satan *(Deut. 30:19)*.

(c) The counselor must recognize the human need for discipline which involves God's guidance and protection.

(d) The counselor must also recognize that many of the problems of the counselee would be solved if the counselee is reconciled to God through Christ.

V. MINISTERING SALVATION

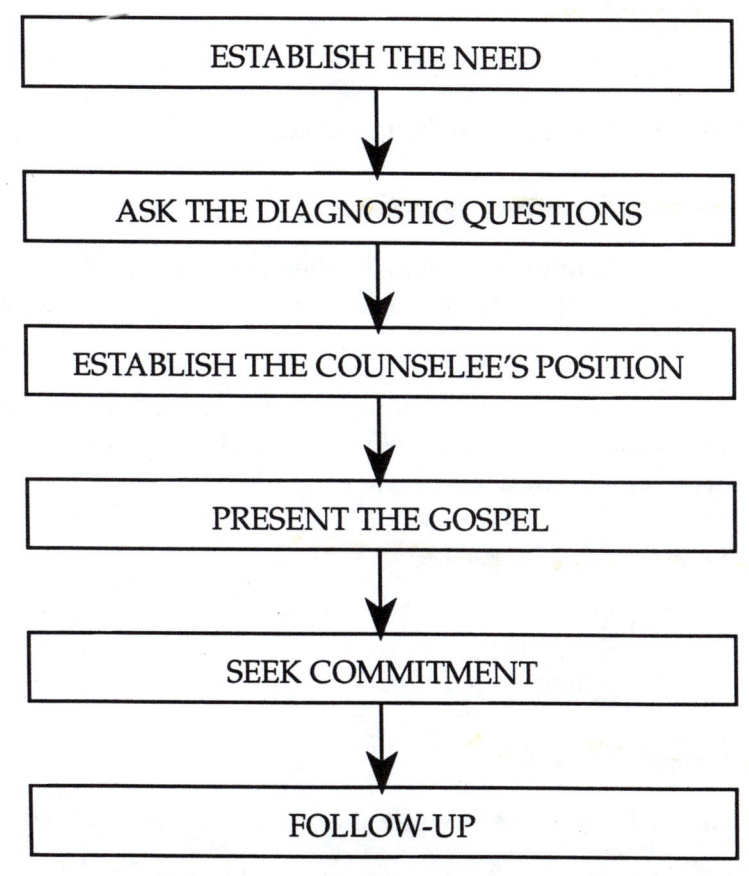

```
┌─────────────────────────────────┐
│      ESTABLISH THE NEED         │
└─────────────────────────────────┘
                 ↓
┌─────────────────────────────────┐
│   ASK THE DIAGNOSTIC QUESTIONS  │
└─────────────────────────────────┘
                 ↓
┌─────────────────────────────────┐
│ ESTABLISH THE COUNSELEE'S POSITION │
└─────────────────────────────────┘
                 ↓
┌─────────────────────────────────┐
│       PRESENT THE GOSPEL        │
└─────────────────────────────────┘
                 ↓
┌─────────────────────────────────┐
│       SEEK COMMITMENT           │
└─────────────────────────────────┘
                 ↓
┌─────────────────────────────────┐
│          FOLLOW-UP              │
└─────────────────────────────────┘
```

James Kennedy, in his popular Evangelism Explosion Program, trains the counselor to ask questions to determine the spiritual need of the person, to present the Gospel to him, to help him to make a commitment to Jesus Christ, and to do immediate follow up with that individual:

A. Establish the Individual's Need Through Directed Conversation

1. The need to know Christ.

2. The need to have a problem solved.

B. Ask the Diagnostic Questions

1. Have you come to the place in your spiritual life where you know for certain that if you were to die tonight you would go to heaven?

2. Suppose you were to die tonight and stand before God and He were to say you, "Why should I let you into My heaven?" What would you say?

C. Establish the Counselee's Position

1. Is he saved?

2. Is he struggling with difficulties? If so, heal these.

D. Present the Gospel

1. Grace: Heaven is a free gift. It is not earned or deserved.

2. Man: Man is a sinner. He cannot save himself.

3. God: God is merciful and therefore does not want to punish us. But God is also just and must punish our sins.

4. Christ: Christ is God-man. He died to pay for our sins and purchased a place in heaven for us.

5. Faith: It is not head knowledge or temporal faith. It is trusting in Jesus alone for our salvation.

E. Seek Commitment

1. Find out whether the Gospel makes sense to him.
2. Invite him to receive the gift of eternal life.
3. Clarify commitment:
    (a) The transferal of trust from himself to Jesus
    (b) Receiving the resurrected and living Christ
    (c) Receiving Christ as Savior and as Lord
    (d) Repentance
    (e) Becoming a responsible member of God's family
4. Say a prayer of commitment.
5. Share with him assurance of salvation.

F. Follow-Up

1. Share the need for:
    (a) Bible study
    (b) Praying always
    (c) Worshiping
    (d) Fellowship
    (d) Witnessing

VI. PRACTICAL

A. Discussion of the main points of the lesson presented.

B. Establish the need for commitment or recommitment in the group.

C. Role play the ministering of Salvation.

LESSON 3

BAPTISM IN THE HOLY SPIRIT

I. WHO THE HOLY SPIRIT IS

Probably the least known member of the Godhead.

WHO IS THE HOLY SPIRIT?

HE IS GOD (Acts 5:3,4)

- Eternal (Hebrews 9:14)
- Omnipresent (Ps. 139:7-10)
- Omniscient (1 Cor. 2:10,11)
- Omnipotent (Luke 1:35)

HE IS A PERSON

- Speaks (Acts 13:2)
- Feels (Eph. 4:30)
- Comforts (Acts 9:31)
- Prays (Romans 8:26)
- Teaches (John 14:26)

A. God

1. Peter told Ananias that lying to the Holy Spirit, was lying to God. "you have not lied to men but to God" *(Acts 5:3,4)*.

2. The Holy Spirit has the characteristics that only God has.

    (a) He is eternal. The blood of Christ through the "Eternal Spirit" will purge our consciences from dead works to serve a living God (Heb. 9:14).

    (b) He is omnipresent. "Where can I go from your Spirit? Or where can I flee from your presence? ...heaven, hell...uttermost parts of the sea... behold You are there" (Ps. 139:7-10).

    (c) He is omniscient. "For what man knows the things of man except the spirit of the man which is in him. Even so no one knows the things of God except the Spirit of God" (1 Cor. 2:10,11).

    (d) He is omnipotent.

The angel prophesied to Mary that the Holy Spirit would come upon her, and the power of the Highest would come upon her, and she would bear a son who would be called the Son of God (Luke 1:35).

B. The Holy Spirit is a Person

1. He has the characteristics of a person.

    (a) He speaks. As Barnabas, Saul, and others fasted, the Holy Spirit spoke to them, asking them to separate to Him Barnabas and Saul for the work to which He had called them *(Acts 13:2)*.

(b) He feels. We are not to grieve the Holy Spirit of God *(Eph. 4:30)*.

(c) He comforts. The churches in Judea, Galilee and Samaria walked "in the fear of the Lord and in the comfort of the Holy Spirit" *(Acts 9:31)*.

(d) He prays. "For we do not know what we ought to pray for as we ought, but the Spirit Himself makes intercession for us with groanings, which can be uttered" *(Rom. 8:26)*.

(e) He teaches. "He will teach you all things" *(John 14:26)*.

II. THE MINISTRY OF THE HOLY SPIRIT

SALVATION (John 3:5)

- Convicts (John 16:8)
- Produces regeneration (Titus 3:5)
- Liberates from power of sin and death (Romans 8:2)
- Delivers from power of the flesh (Romans 8:9)
- Gives assurance of salvation (2 Tim. 1:2)

POWER FOR HOLY LIVING

- Quickens physical body (Romans 8:11)
- Empowers (Micah 3:8)
- Anoints (1 John 2:20)
- Sanctifies (2 Thess. 2:13)
- Gives joy (Romans 14:17)

- Bears fruit in our lives (Gal. 5:22,23)

- Inspires our prayers (Romans 8:26)

- Inspires or praise and worship (John 4:24)

A. Two Steps In the Christian Journey

1. Salvation. "Unless one is born of water and the Spirit, he cannot enter the kingdom of heaven" (John 3:5).

    (a) The Holy Spirit convicts of sin. "And when He has come, He will convict the world of sin, right-eousness, and of judgment" (John 16:8).

    (b) He produces conversion and regeneration. "Not by works of righteousness which we have done, but according to His mercy He saved us, through the washing of regeneration and renewing of the Holy Spirit" (Titus 3:5).

    (c) He liberates from the power of sin and death. "For the law of the Spirit of life in Christ Jesus has made me free from the law of sin and death" (Romans 8:9).

    (d) He delivers from the power of the flesh. "But you are not in the flesh but in the Spirit, if so that the Spirit of God dwells in you" (Rom. 8:9).

    (e) He gives assurance of salvation. "The Spirit Himself bears witness with our spirit that we are children of God" (Rom. 8:16).

2. Power for holy living

    (a) He quickens our physical bodies. "But if the Spirit of Him that raised up Jesus from the dead dwells in you, He who raised up Christ from the dead will also give life to your mortal bodies through His Spirit who dwells in you" (Rom. 8:11).

(b) He empowers us. "But truly I am full of power by the Spirit of the Lord, and of justice and might to declare to Jacob his transgression and to Israel his sin" *(Micah 3:8)*.

(c) He anoints us. "But you have an anointing from the Holy One and you know all things" (1 *John 2:20)*.

(d) He sanctifies us. Paul thanks God for the Thessalonians, for from the beginning God chose them "for salvation through sanctification by the Spirit and belief in the truth" *(2 Thess. 2:13)*.

(e) He gives us joy. "for the kingdom of God is not food and drink, but righteousness and peace and joy in the Holy Spirit" *(Rom. 14:17)*.

(f) He bears fruit in our lives. Love, joy, peace long-suffering, kindness, goodness, faithfulness, gentleness, self-control *(Gal. 5:22,23)*.

(g) He gives gifts *(1 Cor. 12:3-11)*.

Speaking: tongues, interpretation, prophecy

Revelation: wisdom, knowledge, discerning of spirits

Power: miracles, faith, healing.

(h) He inspires our prayers. "for we do not know what we should pray for as we ought, but the Spirit Himself makes intercession for us" *(Rom. 8:26b)*.

(i) He inspires our praise and worship. "God is Spirit and those who worship Him must worship in spirit and truth" (John 4:24).

III. BAPTISM IN THE HOLY SPIRIT

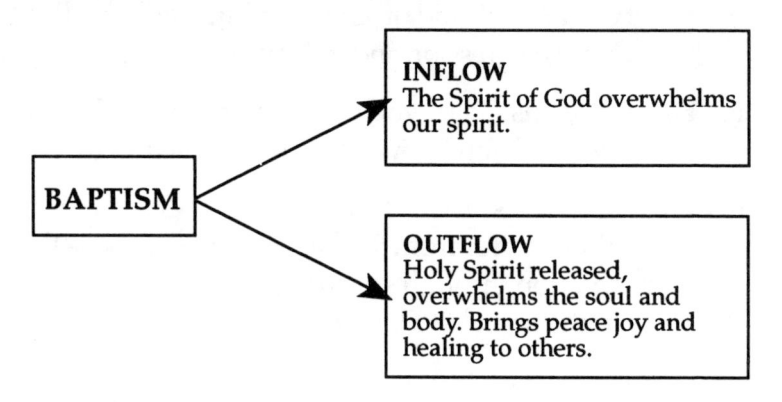

```
                    ┌─────────────────────────────┐
                    │ INFLOW                      │
                  ─▶│ The Spirit of God overwhelms│
                 /  │ our spirit.                 │
┌──────────┐    /   └─────────────────────────────┘
│ BAPTISM  │◀──
└──────────┘    \   ┌─────────────────────────────┐
                 \  │ OUTFLOW                     │
                  ─▶│ Holy Spirit released,       │
                    │ overwhelms the soul and     │
                    │ body. Brings peace joy and  │
                    │ healing to others.          │
                    └─────────────────────────────┘
```

A. Review "The Necessity For the New Birth"

Chart In Lesson II.

B. The Meaning Of Baptism In The Holy Spirit

1. The word "baptism" is from the Greek word "baptizo" meaning to overcome or overwhelm someone or something.

2. The Spirit of God totally overwhelms or baptizes our spirit.

3. There is only one baptism, but two parts. "one Lord, one faith, one baptism" (Eph. 4:5).

4. Jesus is the baptizer. John said of Jesus, "Upon whom you see the Spirit descending, and remaining on Him, this is He who baptizes with the Holy Spirit" *(John 1:33b)*.

5. We receive power to be witnesses for Christ. "But you shall receive power when the Holy Spirit is come upon you; and you shall be witnesses to Me in Jerusalem, and in all Judea and Samaria, and to the end of the earth" (Acts *1:8)*.

6. God promised to pour out His Spirit on all flesh. "And it shall come to pass afterward, that I will pour out My Spirit on all flesh..." (Joel 2:28).

C. Speaking In Tongues

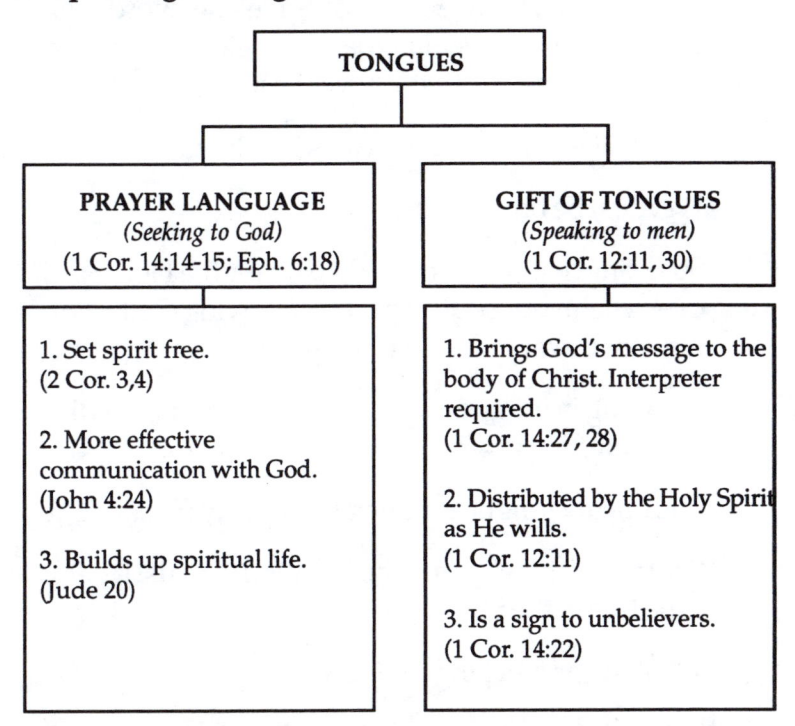

	TONGUES	
PRAYER LANGUAGE *(Seeking to God)* (1 Cor. 14:14-15; Eph. 6:18)		**GIFT OF TONGUES** *(Speaking to men)* (1 Cor. 12:11, 30)
1. Set spirit free. (2 Cor. 3,4) 2. More effective communication with God. (John 4:24) 3. Builds up spiritual life. (Jude 20)		1. Brings God's message to the body of Christ. Interpreter required. (1 Cor. 14:27, 28) 2. Distributed by the Holy Spirit as He wills. (1 Cor. 12:11) 3. Is a sign to unbelievers. (1 Cor. 14:22)

God uses speaking in tongues in two different ways:

1. As a prayer language.

   (a) The following words of Paul indicate that the prayer language or "praying in the Spirit" is for all: "I wish you all spoke with tongues..." *(1 Cor. 14:5a)*. "praying always with all prayer and supplication in the Spirit" *(Eph. 6:18)*.

(b) In Dennis Bennett's book, "How To Pray For The Release Of The Holy Spirit," he makes the following points:

It means we speak to God not using our own words, but trusting the Holy Spirit to "give the words as He chooses, in whatever language He selects - sometimes a brand new tongue that's never been spoken."

No special ability or holiness is involved.

We must be born again.

Speaking in tongues makes a path for the Holy Spirit to overwhelm our soul and body, allowing God a greater influence over our whole being.

Speaking in tongues helps us grow spiritually, edifying us or building us up *(1 Cor. 14:5a; Jude 20).*

The unruly tongue is tamed in this way *(James 3:1-5).*

It is the key to releasing the Holy Spirit in us. It helps us to be free in the Spirit.

(c) What the prayer language does.

It begins to set us free in the Spirit.

It helps us communicate with God in new freedom, and so builds up our spiritual life.

It is a simple, refreshing way to pray, bringing rest to our souls.

It gives us the ability to pray more effectively to get God's will done in the world around us.

Baptism In The Holy Spirit 41

2. As the gift of tongues

After you begin to use your prayer language, you will begin to see much more of the spiritual gifts at work in your life. The Holy Spirit distributes these as He wills: "But one and the same Spirit works all these things, distributing to each as He wills."

(a) The gift of tongues is one of nine spiritual gifts which the Holy Spirit gives to whomever He wills. Paul says, "all don't speak in tongues, do they?" *(1 Cor. 12:30).*

(b) The Holy Spirit gives this gift when God has something to say to His people gathered together. He will let you know when He wants you to speak out in a congregation. If He doesn't, and you speak out, you will only be praying aloud in your prayer language.

(c) If the Spirit moves us to bring a message in tongues, He will provide the interpretation, either through some other person or yourself.

(d) We can control this gift. "And the spirits of the prophets are subject to the prophets" (1 *Cor. 12:30).*

(e) Sometimes the Holy Spirit may speak in a known language - French, Hebrew, etc. Another person understands it.

(f) The gift of tongues is a sign for unbelievers *(1 Cor. 12:30).*

D. The Necessity For Baptism In the Holy Spirit

1. Empowerment for ministry.

- (a) "Jesus told His disciples to wait for the Promise of the Father" and they "shall be baptized with the Holy Spirit not many days from now" (*Acts 1:4,5*).

- (b) They shall receive power to witness. "You shall receive power when the Holy Spirit has come upon you, and you shall be witnesses to Me in Jerusalem, Judea and Samaria and to the end of the earth" (Acts *1:8*).

- (c) Teaching, preaching and witnessing without the anointing accomplishes much less.

2. Speaking in tongues is an integral part of the baptism in the Holy Spirit.

3. We will need to be constantly refilled with the Holy Spirit for each emergency of Christian service.

E. Preparation For Baptism in the Holy Spirit

1. PREPARATION

   (a) Receiving Jesus as Savior

   (b) Checking attitudes

   (c) Checking involvement in cults

   (d) Checking involvement in the occult

2. EARNEST DESIRE (1 Cor. 12:31, 14:1)

3. INVITING JESUS TO BAPTIZE (John 1:33)

4. TAKING A STEP IN FAITH (James 2:20; Ps. 81:10)

5. PRACTICE (Jude 20)

1. Receive Jesus as Savior.

    (a) This is when the Holy Spirit comes to live in us.

    (b) If the individual is not born again, another spirit (evil) living in there can be released when we pray.

    (c) Ask the individual if he remembers a specific time when he received Jesus as Lord and Savior of his life.

2. Check your attitudes.

    (a) Wrong attitudes can block the flow of the Holy Spirit through us: unforgiveness, rebellion, disobedience, carnality. These defile us *(Jude 23)*.

    (b) Confess to God; release to Him; ask His forgiveness; bind and cast out any spirits in this connection.

3. Check for involvement in occultic activities.

    (a) Occultic teaching does not line up with God's Word *(2 Peter 2:4-9)*.

    (b) List some cults: Bahai, Jehovah's Witnesses, Transcendental Meditation, Christian Science, Mormonism, etc.

4. Check for involvement in the occult.

    (a) Occult is supernatural performance through evil power: astrology, hypnotism, magic, witchcraft, mind reading, hand-writing analysis, ouija boards, etc. Evil spirits enter.

    (b) God forbids these *(Deut. 18:10-12)* and says these are to be punishable by death: "You shall not permit a sorceress to live" (Ex. *22:18*).

(c) These must be confessed, released to God, forgiven by God, and any evil spirits bound and cast out. We must renounce all we can remember.

F. Receiving the Baptism In the Holy Spirit

1. Earnestly desire to receive it. The will is the gateway to the spirit. We do not have a gift which we do not accept *(1 Cor. 12:30)*. Pursue love and desire spiritual gifts *(1 Cor. 14:1)*.

2. Invite Jesus to baptize us. He is the baptizer.

"Upon whom you see the Spirit descending and remaining on Him, this is He who baptizes with the Holy Spirit" (John *1:33)*.

3. Take a step in faith. Give Jesus your voice. "Faith without works is dead" *(James 2:20)*.

   (a) Open your mouth and begin to make sounds. One sound can begin to set your spirit free. Talk to God: "Open your mouth wide and I will fill it" *(Ps. 81:10)*.

4. Continue your practice speaking in tongues. It edifies *(Jude 20)*.

IV. PRACTICAL

A. Leading the Counselors Through the Baptism of the Holy Spirit

1. Prepare them for baptism as illustrated above.

2. Lead them through the baptism.

3. Let those already baptized assist by standing behind them and helping to lead them through.

B. Role play by allowing participants to lead each other through this process.

C. Lead counselors through prayers yielding themselves to God and asking for His anointing for ministry.

NOTES

LESSON 4

MARRIAGE AND FAMILY COUNSELING

I. DEFINITION OF MARRIAGE AND FAMILY COUNSELING

A. It Deals With Family Problems

1. Those related to beginning and maintaining a family.

B. It Is a Process in Which a Counselor Helps Persons to Make Plans and Solve Problems

1. Plans and problems are related to courtship, marriage and family relations.

2. The counselor helps individuals, couples or families.

II. MARITAL RELATIONS

A. Components of A Good Marriage

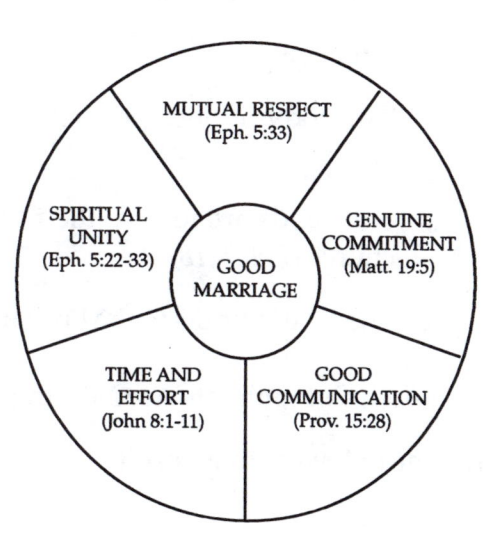

GOOD MARRIAGE

- MUTUAL RESPECT (Eph. 5:33)
- GENUINE COMMITMENT (Matt. 19:5)
- GOOD COMMUNICATION (Prov. 15:28)
- TIME AND EFFORT (John 8:1-11)
- SPIRITUAL UNITY (Eph. 5:22-33)

There are problems when any of these are absent:

1. Mutual respect for each other *(Eph. 6:18)*

    (a) Accept each other

2. Genuine commitment *(Matt. 19:5)*

    (a) Forsake all others

    (b) The two should become one flesh

3. Good communication *(Prov. 15:28)*

    (a) Spend quality time together

    (b) Think before speaking

4. Time and effort *(John 8:1-11)*

    (a) Try to work things out

    (b) Discuss story of the woman caught in adultery

    (c) Be kind and compassionate

5. Spiritual unity

    (a) The body of one spouse belongs to the other *(1 Cor. 12:30)*

    (b) Husbands are to love their wives as Christ loves the church *(Eph. 6:18)*

    (c) The wife submits to the husband *(Eph. 5:22,23)*

B. When Components Are Missing

1. The following may result:

- (a) Mistrust, abuse, conflicts, adultery, divorce, anger, and spiritual adultery (Matt. 19:5)
- (b) Pressure to do wrong in matters of conscience, when we ought to obey God rather than men (Acts 5:29)
- (c) Problem of wife's submission to husband

C. Some Areas Where Counseling Is Required

1. Anticipating Marriage

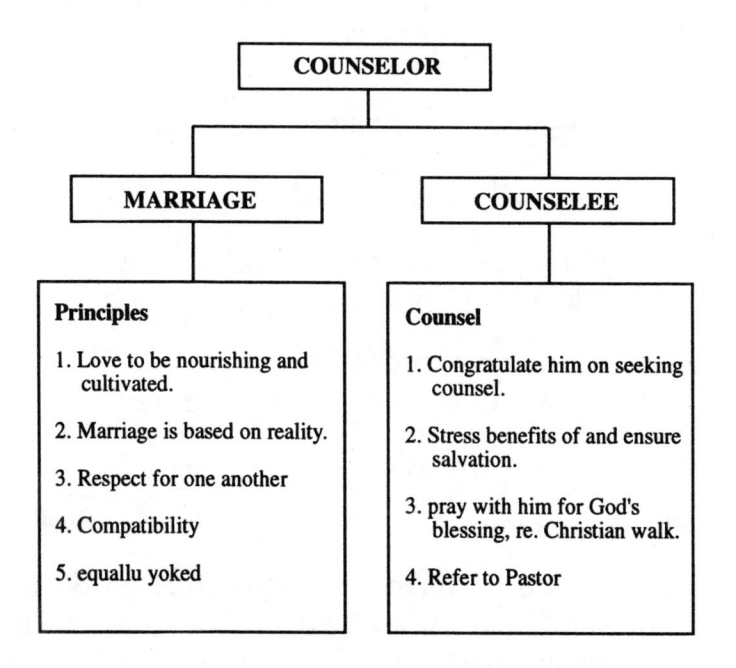

MARRIAGE — Principles	COUNSELEE — Counsel
1. Love to be nourishing and cultivated.	1. Congratulate him on seeking counsel.
2. Marriage is based on reality.	2. Stress benefits of and ensure salvation.
3. Respect for one another	3. pray with him for God's blessing, re. Christian walk.
4. Compatibility	4. Refer to Pastor
5. equallu yoked	

(Under COUNSELOR, branching to MARRIAGE and COUNSELEE)

Some principles for counselor and counselee to understand:

(a) Marriage is the most serious long-term covenant a couple will make in their lifetime. They should be adequately prepared. Some helpful principles are:

(i) Love must be nourished and cultivated. Look to God for guidance.

(ii) Marriage is based on reality. The honeymoon will be over and an unrealistically high expectation will be shattered.

(iii) There must be respect for each other. Each must have a good self image, act with maturity, understand each other as different individuals, and have a solid relationship with Jesus Christ.

(iv) Similarities in partners stand better chance of marriage survival:

- religious; social; cultural; economic level
- stable home situation
- equal educational advantage

(v) Marriage was never intended to be a reform school. Don't help to change the person.

(vi) Marry in the Lord *(1 Cor. 7:39b)*.
Do not be unequally yoked *(2 Cor. 14:1)*.

(b) Advice to the counselee:

(i) Congratulate his initiative in seeking counsel.

(ii) Advise him on the wisdom of seeking God. If not saved, lead him to Christ, and stress the benefits of this in a marriage.

(iii) Pray with the counselee for God's blessings on his practice of Christianity.

(iv) Refer to the Pastor.

D. One Saved Spouse *(1 Cor. 12:3-11)*

1. The saved spouse has the responsibility to remain in the marriage as long as the other spouse is willing to live with him or her.

2. The unbelieving spouse and children are sanctified by the believing one.

3. If the unbeliever departs, the other spouse is under no bondage in such a case.

4. While the couple lives together, there is always hope that the saved one will lead the other to salvation.

5. For the saved spouse the situation is spiritual warfare, and he must pray for the salvation of his or her mate:

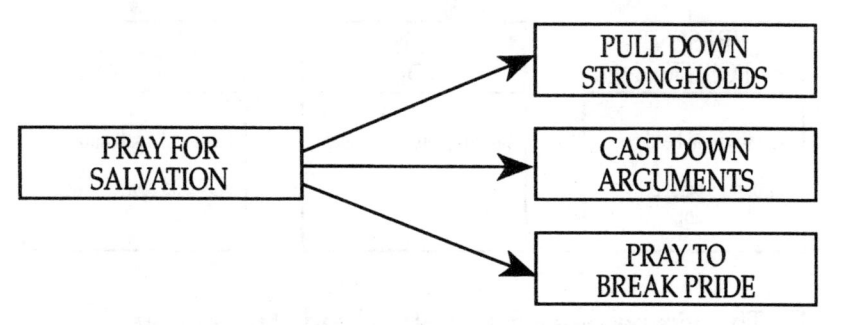

```
                          ┌──────────────────┐
                     ───▶ │ PULL DOWN        │
                          │ STRONGHOLDS      │
┌──────────────┐          └──────────────────┘
│ PRAY FOR     │          ┌──────────────────┐
│ SALVATION    │ ───────▶ │ CAST DOWN        │
│              │          │ ARGUMENTS        │
└──────────────┘          └──────────────────┘
                          ┌──────────────────┐
                     ───▶ │ PRAY TO          │
                          │ BREAK PRIDE      │
                          └──────────────────┘
```

   (a) Pull down strongholds that keeps mate from acknowledging God.

   (i) Ask God to reveal your mate's habits, complexes, or deep-seated problems.

   (ii) Don't mistake manifestation for stronghold.

   (b) Cast down imagination.

   (i) Imagination is wrong thoughts or arguments the unbelieving teach.

- (c) Break their pride.
    - (i) Pray that God would break their pride.
    - (ii) Pride is exalting high things against the knowledge of God.
    - (iii) Pride keeps us from confession.
    - (iv) Be prepared to stand beside your mate when God breaks his pride.
    - (v) Our lives are changed when we pray to God.

E. Saved Wife And Unsaved Husband

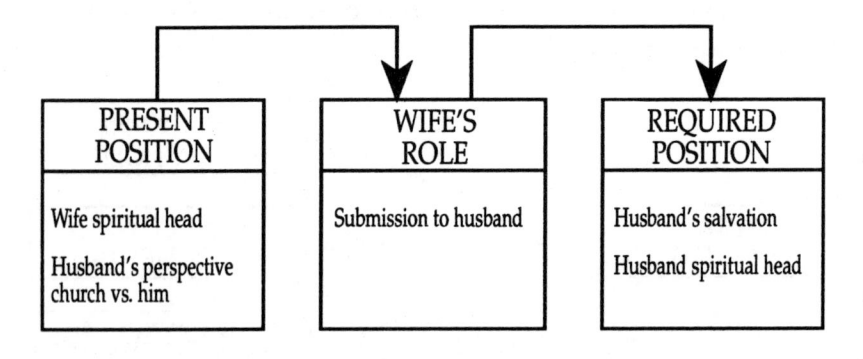

PRESENT POSITION	WIFE'S ROLE	REQUIRED POSITION
Wife spiritual head Husband's perspective church vs. him	Submission to husband	Husband's salvation Husband spiritual head

1. The wife becomes the spiritual head of the family.
2. Wives are to be submissive to their husbands (I Pet. 3:1-5).
    - (a) Even if some husbands do not obey the Word, they, without a word, may be won by the conduct of their wives.
    - (b) Outward adorning is not important, but the wife must have a gentle and quiet spirit, which is very precious in the sight of God.

3. God will use the wife's submission to draw the husband to Himself. When a woman is dead in Christ, submission is not the issue.

4. The issue is the salvation of the husband rather than the submission of the wife.

5. When the wife is the spiritual head, the danger is that the husband sees the church as opposition.

6. The husband is looking for the "hidden person of the heart." He doesn't want to see the wife doing everything for Jesus and nothing for him.

7. When a wife obeys her husband, God works through the obedience of the wife and makes the decisions through the husband that way.

8. The wife must share her body with her husband *(1 Cor. 7:4a)*.

F. Contemplating Divorce

1. Definition of divorce:

It is the legal dissolution of a marriage, and a departure from what God intended, and not endorsed by Scripture except under the following conditions:

(a) Sexual immorality *(Matt. 19:5)*

- committing adultery, homosexuality, or bestiality, and having no intention of repenting or seeking God's forgiveness.

(b) Desertion (1 Cor. 14:1)

- especially when an unbelieving partner deserts a Christian spouse.

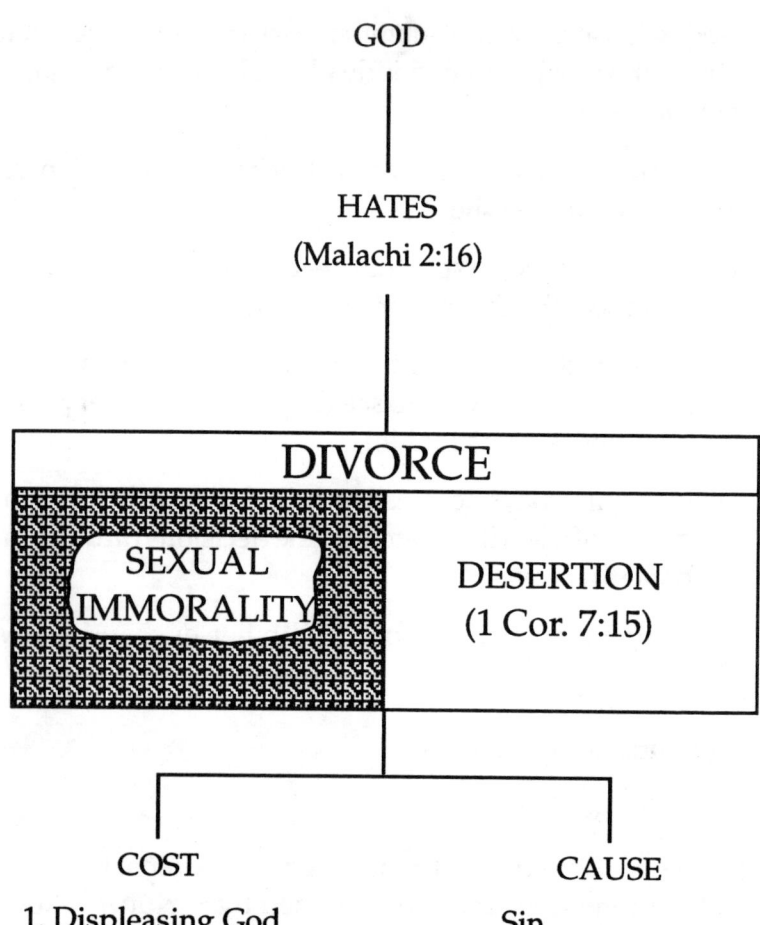

```
                    GOD
                     |
                   HATES
                (Malachi 2:16)
                     |
┌─────────────────────────────────────────┐
│                DIVORCE                  │
├──────────────────┬──────────────────────┤
│     SEXUAL       │     DESERTION        │
│   IMMORALITY     │    (1 Cor. 7:15)     │
└──────────────────┴──────────────────────┘
         │                    │
        COST                CAUSE
```

1. Displeasing God   Sin
2. Disrupting family life   Inflexible will
3. Emotional trauma

2. If married and divorced before coming to Christ, stay with the second wife. Two wrongs don't make a right.

3. Having an unbelieving spouse is no grounds for divorce (1 *Cor. 7:12-16*).

4. The cause of divorce.

(a) Sin in the life of one or both partners.

(b) Inflexible wills (Matt. 19:5)

> Jesus replied, "Moses, because of the hardness of your hearts, permitted you to divorce your wives, but from the beginning it was not so.

5. God is against divorce.

    (a) It covers one's garment with violence (Mal. 2:15,16).

    (b) Husband and wife instructed not to leave each other (1 Cor. 7:10,11).

6. Divorce costs dearly.

    (a) It displeases God (Matt. 2:15,16).

    (b) It disrupts the continuity of life and adversely affects children, parents, and extended family.

    (c) It is an emotionally traumatic experience which may create more problems rather then solving them.

7. Options for solutions.

    (a) Attempt to work things out in all humility and with a forgiving spirit (Matt. 18:21,22).

        (i) Jesus said to forgive up to seventy times seven.

    (b) Submit to counseling with Christian marriage counselor or qualified pastor.

    (c) It may even be advisable, in serious cases of physical or psychological abuse, drunkenness, homosexuality, drugs, etc., to have a trial separation for a while.

G. Counseling Strategy

The Counselor must:

1. Demonstrate loving and caring attitude.
2. Listen attentively; let the counselee ventilate feelings until he has a grasp of the situation.
3. Don't take sides, present scriptural point of view.
4. To ensure help, seek counselee's commitment to Christ, if he or she is not already committed. Counsel on follow-up steps.
5. Encourage counselee to exhaust all options in search of scriptural solution.
6. Pray with him for God's intervention in putting his life and marriage together according to Scripture:

    - Rom. 7:2 - widowhood

    - Prov. 18:22 - finding a wife

    - 1 Cor. 14:1 - unity in marriage

    - 1 Pet. 3:7 - husband/wife relationship.

III. PARENT/CHILD RELATIONSHIP

PARENT'S RESPONSIBILITY

1. Set example
2. Administer discipline
3. Follow through with discipline

4. Apologize and ask forgiveness for mistakes
5. Spend quality time with children

COUNSELING STRATEGY

Stress:

1. Manifestation of the fruit of the Spirit (Gal. 5:22)
2. Salvation of the household (Acts 16:31)
3. Child's obedience to parents
4. Need to renew mind
5. Pray for: Holy Spirit's revelation of problem areas.

Ref.　　1 Cor. 11:1-12　　　Eph. 5:22, 6:4

　　　　Philemon　　　　　Hebrews 12:5-1

　　　　Isaiah　　　　　　Eph. 6:1-3

A. What The Scripture Says

1. Obey God and all will go well with you and your children (Deut. 12:28).
2. Obedience of children to parents pleases God (Col. 3:20).
3. Children are warned not to disobey parents, and fathers warned not to provoke children.

B. The Problem

1. Family relations marred by conflict, rebellion, anxiety, lack of discipline, confusion. The counselee is seeking peace in the home. The Scriptures specifically say:

(a) Teach the children the law (Deut. 6:5-7).

(b) Train up the child in the way he should go (Prov. 22:6).

(c) Fathers must not provoke children to wrath (Eph. 4:5).

2. Parental responsibility:

  (a) To set the example the children should follow.

  (b) To seek the cause of the problem and try to eradicate it.

  (c) To avoid parental disagreement in front of children.

  (d) To be specific in all instructions of discipline.

3. Administering discipline:

  (a) Establish clear guidelines so that the child knows what he is supposed to do or not do.

  (b) Punish disobedience.

  (c) Discipline child in love and not anger.

  (d) Make sure the child knows what he has done wrong.

  (e) Always express forgiveness afterwards, then treat the child as if it never happened.

  (f) Follow through with discipline making sure your commands are obeyed.

  (g) If you make a mistake, apologize and ask forgiveness of the child. Remember, nothing will substitute for spending time with the child. Neglect of the above is the cause of many hang-ups experienced in adulthood.

C. Counseling Strategy

1. Emphasize the need to manifest the fruit of the Spirit (Gal. 5:22,23).

2. Assist parents in believing and claiming the promise in Acts 16:31: "Believe on the Lord Jesus Christ, and you will be saved, you and your household."

3. To the child counselee, emphasize the necessity for obedience to parents, since this is an instruction from the Word of God. Parents, also have the responsibility to lead their children in the way of the Lord (Col. 3:20,21). Disobedience causes confusion in the home.

4. Emphasize the need for renewing the mind:

    (a) Discuss Gal. 5:22.

    (b) Talk through the following Scripture references: 2 Cor. 14:1; Col. 3:10; Rom. 12:2.

    (c) Emphasize the need to give God preeminence in all matters of relationship.

5. Pray with counselee that the Holy Spirit would give discernment about the problem areas. Ask God to reveal to the counselee his role in effecting a solution.

6. Other Scripture references for further study:

    - Divine order in the home (1 Cor. 12:3-11; Eph. 5:22 - 6:4; Col. 3:16-21).

    - Relationships restored in Christ (Philemon).

    - Fasting to restore relationship (Isa. 58).

- Guidance for parents (Prov. 13:24; 29:15; 19:18; Heb. 12:5-11).

- Guidance for children (Eph. 6:1-3).

IV. PRACTICAL

A. Ask for a volunteer to share one family problem from among participants of the workshop. Discuss possible solutions.

B. Form prayer partners, each praying for the family related problem of the other or someone known to him.

LESSON 5

YOUTH COUNSELING

I. THE CHILDREN AND YOUTH THAT WE COUNSEL

A. Human Behavior

Clyde M. Narramore in his book, "Counseling Youth", perceives human behavior to be quite fascinating. While every person behaves differently, the behavior of youth is particularly fascinating, and with youth, the unexpected is most often normal. He sees it as a stage where:

- personalities are forming,

- values are being considered,

- relationships are growing,

- a personal relationship with Jesus is often formed.

1. According to Narramore, the following are some of the premises basic to the understanding of human behavior:

    (a) All behavior is caused. There is a history of experience or a story behind everything we do: e.g.

- crying infant who is hungry or needs physical comfort

- a teenager attending a multitude of social functions indicates need for acceptance

(b) The causes are multiple.

Man is a tripartite being, therefore he has needs of his body, soul, and spirit.

    (i) Physical - need for food, shelter, and sex.

    (ii) Psychological or emotional - the need to belong, achieve, and to be free from guilt and blame.

    (iii) Spiritual - the need for an abiding faith in God. Personalities are never fully developed unless they have experiences developing faith.

Physical, psychological, and spiritual problems overlap, and one can influence the other, e.g., an emotional problem such as bedwetting, can manifest itself physically, and may be caused by tension in the home, anxiety, parental instability, or criticism. Physical causes must be treated physically; psychological causes treated psychologically; and spiritual causes, spiritually.

(c) Developmental factors: There is normal behavior for various age levels, and we need to examine this statement more closely. Narramore lists some characteristics and interests peculiar to the different age groups.

    (i) Age 6 - 9 years

- These children are basically dependent and look to parents for help.

- They are developing their thinking processes.

- They are acquiring a language.

- They are learning the rules of the culture in which they are growing up, and learning their sex roles so that they can be socialized creatures.

- This age group has certain behavior characteristics peculiar to it. Discuss these from the list headed "Behavior Characteristics - Age 6-9 years" on page 64.

(ii) Age 10 - 13 years

- These children are continuing to develop their abilities and have greater resources at their disposal.

- This is the preadolescent stage where individuals are striving for independence and do not easily admit that they need help.

- They need your support in times of dependence. Private counseling can help to resolve conflicts and lead them closer to Christ.

- Characteristics and interests of this age group are found on page 65. Discuss this list.

(iii) Teens

- These young people are more independent, but they need opportunities to mature.

- They need to make mistakes and learn.

- Their emotions are unstable and they need guidance and direction, but will not accept such if given in a domineering and authoritative manner.

YOUTH COUNSELING
BEHAVIOR CHARACTERISTICS
AGE 6-9 YEARS

PHYSICAL AND EMOTIONAL	INTERESTS AND NEEDS
1. Slower growth	1. Some dependence and encouraging support
2. Large muscles better developed	2. Learning situation with concrete objects
3. Tremendous energy, easily fatigued	3. Warmth and encouragement from adults
4. Impulsive	4. More experience to satisfy growing interest
5. Short attention span	5. Physical activity
6. Family ties first separated, school relationships	6. Considerate answers to questions re. physiological changes
7. Less dependence on mother	7. Opportunities to discuss respect for property, and others
8. No discrimination socially	8. Reasonable explanations
9. Sense of right and wrong developing	9. Participation in committee, construction, and dramatic work
10. Often careless and untidy	10. Some quiet activities
11. Concepts of time, money, and distance developing	11. Belonging to a peer group
12. Abstract thinking developing	12. Identification with parent adult of same sex
13. Greater desire for freedom	
14. Very little concern over future	
15. Acquiring basic reading and writing skills	

YOUTH COUNSELING
BEHAVIOR CHARACTERISTICS
AGE 10-13 YEARS

PHYSICAL AND EMOTIONAL	INTERESTS AND NEEDS
1. Steady then rapid growth	1. Inclusion in family and school planning
2. Marked differences in size	2. Knowledge re. maturational differences between boys and girls
3. Girls commonly larger than boys	
4. Onset of secondary sex characteristics	3. Some close friends
	4. Recognition for efforts put forth
5. Girls mature earlier than boys	5. Opportunity to make some decisions
6. Interested in gangs, clubs, teams	6. Girls need menstruation information
7. Strong sense of justice	
8. Can concentrate for longer periods	7. Opportunity to earn and spend money
9. Desirous of group approval	8. Social activities
10. Transition from childhood to adolescence	9. Activities fostering spiritual growth
11. Voice changes may begin in boys	10. Adults in whom to confide
	11. Intellectual challenges at own level
12. Sense of humor developing	12. Understanding of physical and emotional changes

YOUTH COUNSELING
BEHAVIOR CHARACTERISTICS
TEENAGERS

PHYSICAL AND EMOTIONAL	INTERESTS AND NEEDS
1. Sexual maturation, physical and emotional changes	1. Adequate physical appearance
2. Awkward period followed by grace and coordination	2. Acceptance by peer group
3. Increase in muscular strength	3. Vocational guidance
4. Wanting to earn wages	4. Knowledge and understanding of healthy sex relationships
5. Girls desiring to be strong and healthy	5. Assurance of security
6. Seeking independence	6. Independence
7. Developing social abilities	7. Provision for constructive recreation
8. Family relationships may be strained	8. Strong solidarity in family
9. Interested in opposite sex	9. Wholesome activities for bound less energy
10. Seeking adult equality	10. Encouraging development in religious faith
11. Concerned above spirituality and destiny	11. Opportunities for creative activities
	12. Opportunities to increase in knowledge

- They have a well developed sense of morality and justice and know the consequences of their actions.

- They have the ability to take responsibility for their actions. It is often good to bring parents into the counseling relationship, but it is not always needed.

- The counselor's ministry can have deep and lasting value.

Characteristics and interests of this age group are on page 66. Discuss the list.

II. PHYSICAL AND EMOTIONAL CHARACTERISTICS, INTERESTS AND NEEDS

All children and adolescents go through the same stages, but not at the same rate. The wise counselor will consider the behavior and see how best to help them.

A. Problems of Children and Youth

Problems will cover a wide range of physical, emotional, social, and spiritual maladjustments. As the counselor counsels, he should keep in mind four questions:

1. Is the behavior normal for this age level?
2. Does the problem involve other young people?
3. Are there established policies and procedures to be followed?
4. Should there be communication with parents, and who should be responsible for it?

B. Symptomatic Behavior In Youth (See chart on page 69)

The problems that youth experience in their struggle to grow up are manifested in every area of their lives. They are affected physically, emotionally, and spiritually, as they struggle to find their identity, as they strive to develop social abilities, as the sexual maturation process goes on, and as they struggle for independence. The following are some manifested symptomatic behavior:

1. Anger, Hostility

    (a) Problem: Rebellion manifested as:

    - defying rules and regulations

    - argumentative and uncooperative spirits

    - disobedience

    - insubordination

    - deterioration of their general performance

    (b) Caused by:

    - a feeling of insecurity or not being wanted

    - parental rejection

    - broken homes where people have missed out on basic emotional needs

    - conflict in the home

    - poor discipline

    - the individual does not know what to do

    - lack of spiritual conversion and growth. Man's sinful nature versus the nature of Christ.

SYMPTOMATIC BEHAVIOR

BEHAVIOR	PROBLEM	CAUSE
1. Anger, hostility	Rebellion	Insecurity
2. Masturbation, homosexulaity, unnatural sex acts	Sex	Feeling of sexual inadequacy
3. Withdrawal and shyness	Reticence	Shy or over-protective parents
4. Bedwetting beyond the age of 4 years	Bedwetting	Emotional stress
5. Silly actions	Trying to get attention	Lack of attention
6. Dating indiscriminately	Rebellion and frustration	Lack of information and rigid parental contral
7. Provocative dressing	Dressing and grooming	Peer pressure or status keeping
8. Purposelessness	Educational and vocational planning	No Holy Spirit control
9. Backsliding	Spiritual	Returning to non-Christian environment

2. Unnatural sex acts

    (a) Problem: Sex manifested as:

    - homosexuality

    - masturbation

    - pornography

    - promiscuity

    (b) Caused by:

    - feeling of sexual inadequacy

    - dominant mother belittling son's masculinity

    - overly close relationship with someone of the same sex

    - glandular disturbances

    - weak father, overindulgent mother, cruel parents

3. Withdrawal and shyness

    (a) Problem: Reticence manifested as:

    - being silent in company

    - failing to speak out on an issue, even though it may affect them

    - desiring to be alone

    - hating the lime-light

(b) Caused by:

- shy or overprotective parents
- lack of opportunities for social contact
- having their problems go unnoticed for many years

4. Bed-wetting beyond the age of 4 years

   (a) Problem: Bedwetting manifested as:

   - bed-wetting beyond the age of four years

   (b) Caused by:

   - emotional stress
   - tense home setting
   - parental instability
   - bickering and criticism
   - rejection

5. Silly or ostentatious actions

   (a) Problem: Trying to get attention manifested as:

   - outlandish attire
   - efforts to be in the forefront
   - mischief-making
   - playing pranks at the expense of another
   - disruptive behavior
   - attempting to be the center of attention

(b) Caused by:

- lack of attention and affection at home

- parents being over-indulgent or insecure, and allowing children to show off

- a feeling of being unloved

6. Dating indiscriminately or at too early an age

Boys and girls want to know more about each other and how to give as well as receive love. They need guidance and good examples.

(a) Problem: Rebellion and frustration manifested as:

- frustration and rebellion when denied requests to date

(b) Caused by:

- too rigid, or inadequate parental control

- lack of information on the causes of his feeling, the reasoning behind his parent's attitude to dating age, information on petting, going steady, dating the unsaved, and what God's Word says about how we relate to one another

- peer pressure

- inability to establish satisfying relationships with other young persons

- not knowing Christ

7. Provocative dressing

    (a) Problem: Dressing and grooming manifested as:

      - improper and inadequate dressing

    (b) Caused by:

      - desire for status keeping
      - feelings of anger and rebelliousness
      - feelings of inadequacy in their feminine or sexual role
      - lack of parental guidance
      - desire to be accepted by peer group
      - lack of spiritual dedication

8. Purposelessness

    (a) Problem: Lack of educational and vocational planning manifested as:

      - frustration
      - job hopping
      - lack of motivation
      - no plans for the future

    (b) Caused by:

      - lack of Holy Spirit control
      - lack of opportunities for career planning
      - no exposure to areas of his interest

9. Backsliding

   (a) Problem: Spiritual manifested as:

      - decreasing interest in the things of God

      - increasing interest in the things of the world

      - avoidance of friends who would edify

   (b) Caused by:

      - returning to a non-Christian environment

      - failure to study the word of God, share Him, pray, fellowship with other Christians

III. COUNSELING THE YOUTH

A. A Discussion Of The Following Techniques To Be Used In Counseling Youth Problems:

1. Allow the counselee to talk about his underlying problems without too many interruptions.

2. Be a good listener and help him occasionally by means of some open-ended questions.

3. Do not be judgmental.

4. Pray silently and not visibly while the counselee speaks, asking the Holy Spirit to show you the things that you need to minister to, and how to minister to them.

5. Summarize the counselee's statement to make sure that you understand what he has shared with you.

6. Help him to understand the real cause of his problem.

7. Help him to accept responsibility for it.
8. Lead him to Christ.
9. Lead him to reconcile broken relationships.
10. Help him to seek practical solutions for his problems.
11. Introduce him to what the Word of God says on this matter.
12. Refer the counselee if necessary.

IV. PRACTICAL

- **A. Ask for a volunteer to share a youth's problem, and discuss it in open class, attempting to find practical solutions for the problem.**
- **B. Divide the participants into groups of four, letting each group choose a youth problem and discuss the ramifications. End by letting one person out of each group lead the prayer, while others agree.**

NOTES

LESSON 6

CRISIS COUNSELING

I. DEFINITION OF CRISIS

A. A Stage In a Sequence of Events At Which the Trend of Future Events Is Determined:

1. It demands decisive action that will have significant consequences, sometimes life-shaking effects.

2. It requires change.

3. It may be either real or imagined.

4. The emotional impact will be the same if real or imagined.

B. Elements of Crisis

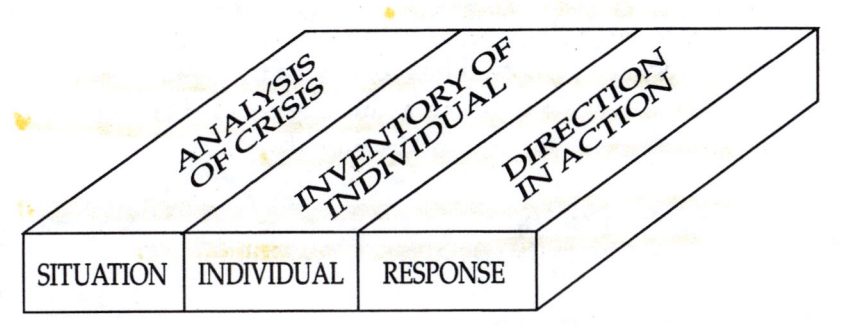

SITUATION	INDIVIDUAL	RESPONSE
ANALYSIS OF CRISIS	INVENTORY OF INDIVIDUAL	DIRECTION IN ACTION

1. The situation - real or imagined, analyze the crisis to arrive at the situation.

2. The individual - acquire further information by taking an inventory of the individual.

3. The response - this is arrived at after examining all the facts and making a decision regarding the direction in which action must be taken.

C. **The Crisis As A Level of Need**

1. Review the levels of need from the chart entitled "Human Difficulties" in Lesson 1.

2. The level of need determines the urgency with which assistance must be given, and the manner we must proceed:

   (a) The problem - this is the lowest level of need and it has a solution.

   (b) The predicament - the problem has been allowed to become complex and there is no easy solution.

   (c) Crisis - this is the turning point of a situation requiring a decision so that a change could be made. It needs immediate and urgent action.

   (d) Panic - the situation has reached a point where it produces overwhelming fear and the person becomes disoriented, hysterical, and irrational.

   (e) Shock - a sudden and violent disturbance of the mind which causes it to lapse for minutes and hours.

D. **Some Crisis Situations**

   - miscarriage, stillbirth, early infant death

   - kidnapping of loved one

Crisis Counseling

- children with terminal illnesses
- releasing a child for adoption
- abortion
- rape
- divorce
- masectomy, disfigurement, amputation, disability
- boy/girl friend situations
- death of spouse
- accidental injuries
- unfaithfulness of spouse
- loss of material goods
- teenage pregnancy
- suicide

II. COUNSELING THOSE IN CRISIS

A. An Important Goal of Counseling

To administer first aid, or bring temporary relief, so that there will be no pressure to act in circumstances where there may not be sufficient information to make wise decisions. This will allow time for more comprehensive and sophisticated counseling later.

B. The Counselor's Responsibility

1. Analysis of crisis situation

    (a) Counselor should help counselee to make biblical analysis of the crisis situation.

    (i) Counselee often feels:

    - frustrated: "I don't know where to begin."

    - overwhelmed: "I can't cope."

    - worried: "It's unreal to be able to do it."

    - unfairly treated: "Why me?"

    (b) Introduce God in the situation

    (i) Limit the crisis by acknowledging God as sovereign over it. The situation is not hopeless, or out of control. If God is in the situation, there's meaning to the crisis (Rom. 8:28).

    (ii) God has allowed a trial (1 Cor. 10:13).

    - no trial is unique

    - every trial is uniquely fitted to each Christian

    - God will deliver His children from the trial

    - there is adequate strength and wisdom meet the trial if God is in it (Phil. 4:13)

C. Analysis of the Crisis Situation (See chart on next page)

1. The five activities of the analysis

Crisis Counseling 81

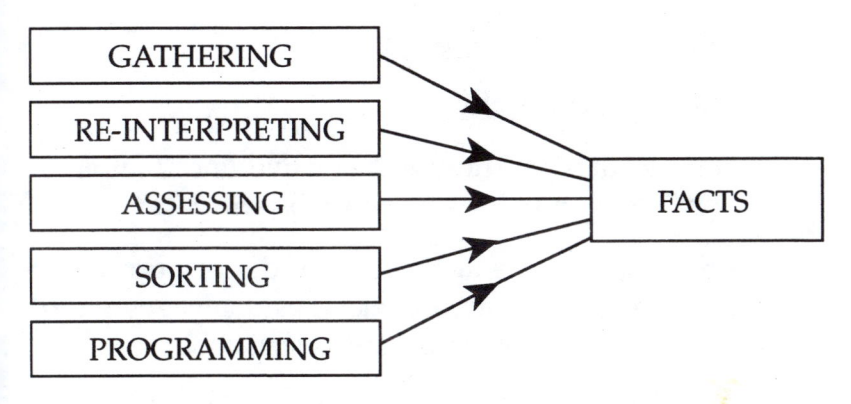

```
┌─────────────────┐
│   GATHERING     │──────┐
├─────────────────┤      │
│ RE-INTERPRETING │──────┤
├─────────────────┤      │      ┌─────────┐
│   ASSESSING     │──────┼─────▶│  FACTS  │
├─────────────────┤      │      └─────────┘
│    SORTING      │──────┤
├─────────────────┤      │
│  PROGRAMMING    │──────┘
└─────────────────┘
```

(a) Gathering the facts:

- about the persons and how they are involved in crisis
- the relationship of counselee to each person and his responsibility to each
- the kind of issues that have emerged

Ask questions:

- what happened?
- what have you done about it so far?
- what do you want me to do?

(b) Re-interpreting the facts:

- the counselee has already put some interpretation on these
- don't call sin sickness
- seek true clarification

(c) Assessing the facts:

(i) Simple versus complex issues

(ii) Immediate concerns

(iii) Truth versus falsity

(d) Sorting out facts: Throw out tentative, uncertain, emotional, conjectured, speculated or bizarre data.

(e) Programming the facts: Put in order of priority for action. The Christian counselor must analyze every crisis situation, to get a grasp on the facts about it:

G = Gathering facts

R = Re-interpreting facts

A = Assessing facts

S = Sorting facts

P = Programing the facts

D. Inventory Of The Individual's State, Attitude, And Behavior (See chart on next page)

In taking a personal inventory of the individual in the crisis, the counselor should remain alert to five key factors:

1. The counselee's state:

   - is he in good possession of his faculties?

   - is he Christian or non-Christian (2 Thess. 4:13)?

   - is he under the influence of drugs or alcohol? (Medical assistance may be needed.)

   - is he emotionally supercharged, hallucinating?

   - is he bitter, resentful, angry? (He needs help to change this. If the counselor is calm and confident, he can have a powerful influence on the counselee.)

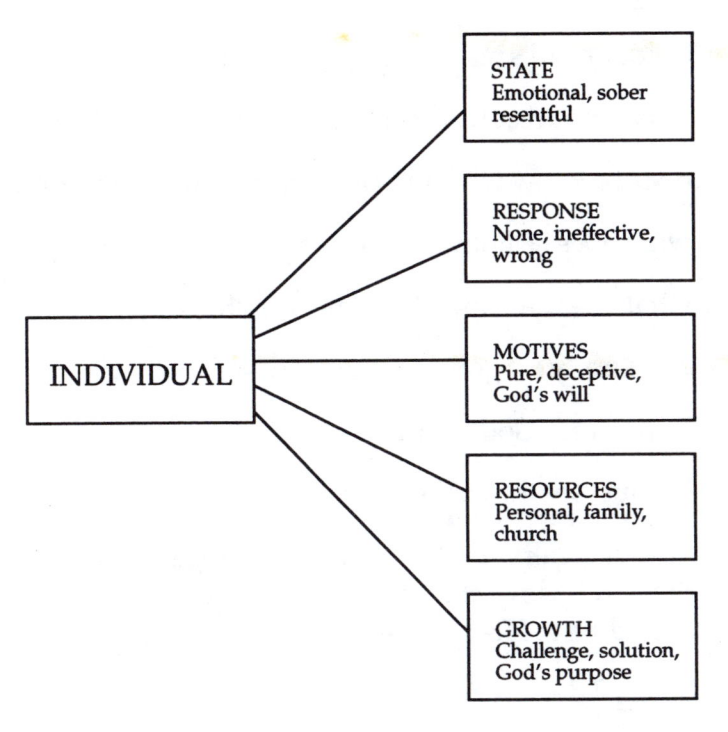

```
                    ┌─────────────────┐
                    │ STATE           │
                    │ Emotional, sober│
                    │ resentful       │
                    └─────────────────┘
                    ┌─────────────────┐
                    │ RESPONSE        │
                    │ None, ineffective,│
                    │ wrong           │
                    └─────────────────┘
┌────────────┐      ┌─────────────────┐
│ INDIVIDUAL │──────│ MOTIVES         │
│            │      │ Pure, deceptive,│
└────────────┘      │ God's will      │
                    └─────────────────┘
                    ┌─────────────────┐
                    │ RESOURCES       │
                    │ Personal, family,│
                    │ church          │
                    └─────────────────┘
                    ┌─────────────────┐
                    │ GROWTH          │
                    │ Challenge, solution,│
                    │ God's purpose   │
                    └─────────────────┘
```

2. **The counselee's response:**

   - has the counselee made the situation a little more complex, e.g., repaying unfaithfulness with unfaithfulness?

   - has he received wrong counseling?

   - has he done nothing?

   - has he become discouraged by his attempts?

3. **The counselee's motives:**

   - what were his motives in doing what he did?

   - were they pure or deceptive?

   - were they in God's will?

4. The counselee's resources:

    - what resources has he to meet crisis?

    - does he know what they are and how to use them?

    - what does he know about his family?

    - what does he know about his church?

5. Opportunity for growth through crisis:

    - he must see God's purpose

    - he must see the challenge in it

    - he must realize that all things work together for good to those who love the Lord and those who are the called according to His purpose.

    - he must defeat crisis

    - he must know that there is a solution to every problem, e.g., widow begins new life as challenge.

E. Direction in Responding to Crisis Issues (See chart on next page)

1. This is the marshaling of all information gleaned, and making decisions to act.

    (a) Action is the key to resolving crisis.

    (b) The decision not to act, is in itself an action.

    (c) Direction is important because:

(i) It is a second opinion from someone more distant from the situation.

(ii) The counselee's emotions sometimes mobilize all bodily faculties.

(iii) A personal presence is important.

(iv) It brings structured control to the person and the situation.

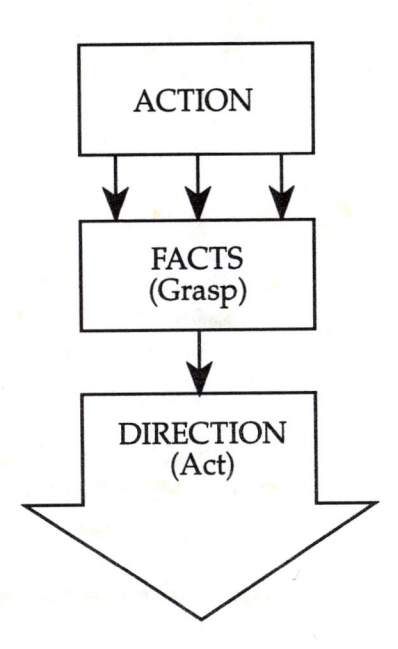

```
ACTION
  ↓↓↓
FACTS
(Grasp)
  ↓
DIRECTION
(Act)
```

2. Types of action:

(a) Authoritative:

- the authoritative use of the Word of God, e.g., call sin, sin.

- the messenger derives authority from the message

- the meaning of the Bible passage must be clearly understood by the counselee

- the counselee needs to know that there is something immovable, the Word of God.

(b) Concrete:

- don't talk in abstract terms. Spell out what is meant, e.g., "considerations" and "inconsiderations" are abstractions. Instead, work on putting shoes back in closets, or the top back on the toothpaste.

- develop list of things to do, e.g., "forgiveness" is abstract. Work on "not bringing things up all the time", or "remembering the sin no more." These exercises should help point the counselee in the direction to apply the Scriptures to solving his own problems.

(c) Tentative:

- some directions are preliminary when the state of the counselee is not conducive to counseling e.g. Counselee is drunk and needs to be sobered up, or the O.D. patient needs to be hospitalized.

- some directions are postponed: decisions in large matters e.g. Grieving widow should not decide to sell the business.

- some directions are preparatory; legitimate work or activity that does not commit one, but leads to biblical disposition of the issues.

- relates to long-term objectives, e.g. preparations of lists

III. A CRISIS COUNSELING FORMAT

A. The Format (See chart on next page)

1. Introduce God in the situation.

    (a) Discuss God's purpose.

    (b) See this as a trial.

2. Biblical analysis of the crisis situation.

G = gathering facts on persons, issues, and relationships
R = re-interpreting facts
A = assessing facts
S = sorting facts
P = programming facts.

3. Inventory of individual

   - his state

   - his response

   - his motives

   - his resources

   - his opportunity for growth.

4. Biblical directions in responding to the issues:

   - authoritative

   - concrete

   - tentative.

A CRISIS COUNSELING FORMAT

1. INTRODUCE GOD IN THE SITUATION

   Purpose

   The Trial

2. ANALYSIS OF THE CRISIS SITUATION

   Gathering

   Re-interpreting

Assessing

Sorting

Programming

3. INVENTORY OF INDIVIDUAL

State

Response

Motives

Resources

Opportunity for growth

4. DIRECTION IN RESPONSE TO ISSUES

Authoritative

Concrete

Tentative

IV. PRACTICAL

A. Let the class provide a crisis situation by completing: "The telephone rings. A desperate voice begs you to come over immediately - a crisis has occurred..." Let the class complete this story.

B. Discuss this situation in class and let them provide possible solutions.

C. Let the class role play the same situation after the discussion.

LESSON 7

PHYSICAL HEALING

I. THE GIFTS OF HEALING (1 COR. 12:4-10)

A. Healing As A Spiritual Gift (1 Cor. 12:4-10)

1. Types of healing:

    (a) Body or physical healing (Matt. 4:23)

    (b) Soul or psychological healing (Mic. 6:13)

    (c) Spiritual healing (Is. 6:10)

2. Healing, like all other spiritual gifts is manifested through the same Holy Spirit.

3. It is given to the individual for the profit of all.

B. Healing is God's Will for Us

1. The theme of healing runs through both the Old and New Testaments of the Bible:

    - Hezekiah, Miriam, Elijah

    - The paralytic, the demon possessed mute man, Lazarus.

2. Jesus ministered healing to the sick and afflicted.

3. Jesus has passed that authority on to us (John 14:12-14).

II. THE CAUSES OF SICKNESS

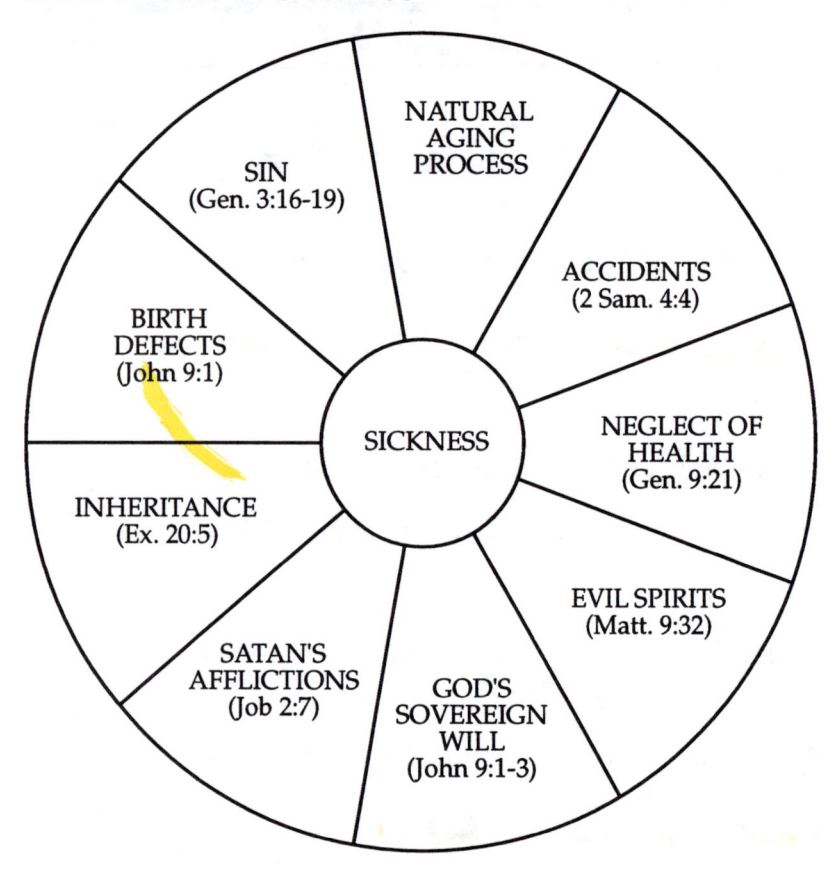

Sickness (center), with causes arranged around it:
- NATURAL AGING PROCESS
- SIN (Gen. 3:16-19)
- BIRTH DEFECTS (John 9:1)
- INHERITANCE (Ex. 20:5)
- SATAN'S AFFLICTIONS (Job 2:7)
- GOD'S SOVEREIGN WILL (John 9:1-3)
- EVIL SPIRITS (Matt. 9:32)
- NEGLECT OF HEALTH (Gen. 9:21)
- ACCIDENTS (2 Sam. 4:4)

A. Sin (Gen. 3:16-19; 1 Cor. 11:27-30)

1. Initially, Adam and Eve's sin brought death and decay to all God's earthly creations.

2. Today, guilt, lack of giving, and taking communion unworthily are still causing illness.

B. Accidents (2 Sam. 4:4)

1. Not necessarily the consequence of wrong doing.

C. Neglect of Health (Gen. 9:21; Luke 21:34)

1. Obesity and indulgence in harmful drinks
2. Inadequate rest
3. Lack of exercise
4. Substance abuse

D. Evil Spirits (Matt. 9:32)

1. Jesus' healing of the mute and demon-possessed man.
2. Some diseases caused by evil spirits:
   (a) Epilepsy
   (b) Scoliosis
   (c) Addiction
   (d) Deafness

E. Birth Defects (John 9:1)

1. Club feet
2. Hydrocephalis (water on the brain)
3. Heart problems
4. Blindness, etc.

F. Inheritance (Ex. 20:5)

1. Diabetes
2. Allergies

3. Bunions
4. Cleft plate

G. Natural Aging Process (Ecc. 12:1-7)

1. Deteriorating organs
2. Tiredness

H. Satan's Afflictions (Job 2:7)

I. God's Sovereign Will (John 9:1-3)

1. That the works of God should be revealed in him.

III. WHY WE ARE SENT TO HEAL THE SICK

A. Jesus' Motives For Healing: (See chart on next page)

1. That it might be fulfilled which was spoken by the prophet Isaiah.

   "He Himself took our infirmities and bore our sickness" (Matt. 8:16,17).

2. To express His compassion.

   "He was moved with compassion for them and healed their sicknesses" (Matt. 14:14).

3. To convey the mercy of God.

   Epaphroditus "was sick almost unto death; but God had mercy on him" (Phil. 2:27).

MOTIVES FOR HEALING

JESUS HEALED:

1. That Isaiah's prophecy may be fulfilled (Matt. 8:16-17)
2. To express His compassion (Matt. 14:14)
3. To convey the mercy of God (Phil. 2:27)
4. To prove that God has truly sent Him (Acts 2:22)
5. To destroy the work of the devil (1 John 3:8)
6. To manifest the works of God (John 9:1-4)
7. To manifest the glory of God (John 11:40)

4. To prove that God had truly sent Him.

   Peter spoke of Jesus, "a Man attested by God to you by miracles, wonders and signs which God did through Him in your midst, as you yourselves also know" (Acts 2:22).

5. To destroy the work of the devil.

   "For this purpose the Son of God was manifested, that He might destroy the works of the devil" (1 John 3:8b).

6. To manifest the works of God.

   The blindness of a man blind from birth was not caused by sin. It was to manifest the works of God (John 9:1-4).

7. To manifest the glory of God.

   Raising Lazarus from the dead after four days, Jesus said to Martha, "Did I not say to you that if you would believe you would see the glory of God?" (John 11:40)

IV. GOD'S PROVISION FOR THE MANIFESTATION OF HIS HEALING POWER

A. Avenues of Healing

1. Intercession (Num. 12:1-14) (See chart on next page)

   (a) Miriam and Aaron spoke against Moses' Ethiopian wife, because they were jealous that God spoke through Moses. God commanded the three of them to step outside the tabernacle of meeting, and he came down in a cloud, striking Miriam with leprosy.

   (b) Moses interceded for Miriam and she was healed. We can stand in the gap for the sick today, and they don't even have to be there.

2. Repentance (1 Kings 13:1-6)

   (a) King Jereboam's hand was withered when he stretched it out against the man of God who cried out against the altar at Bethel, the center of idolatry.

   (b) Jereboam repented and asked the man of God to pray for the restoration of his hand. He did, and God healed Jereboam's hand.

AVENUES AND METHODS FOR HEALING

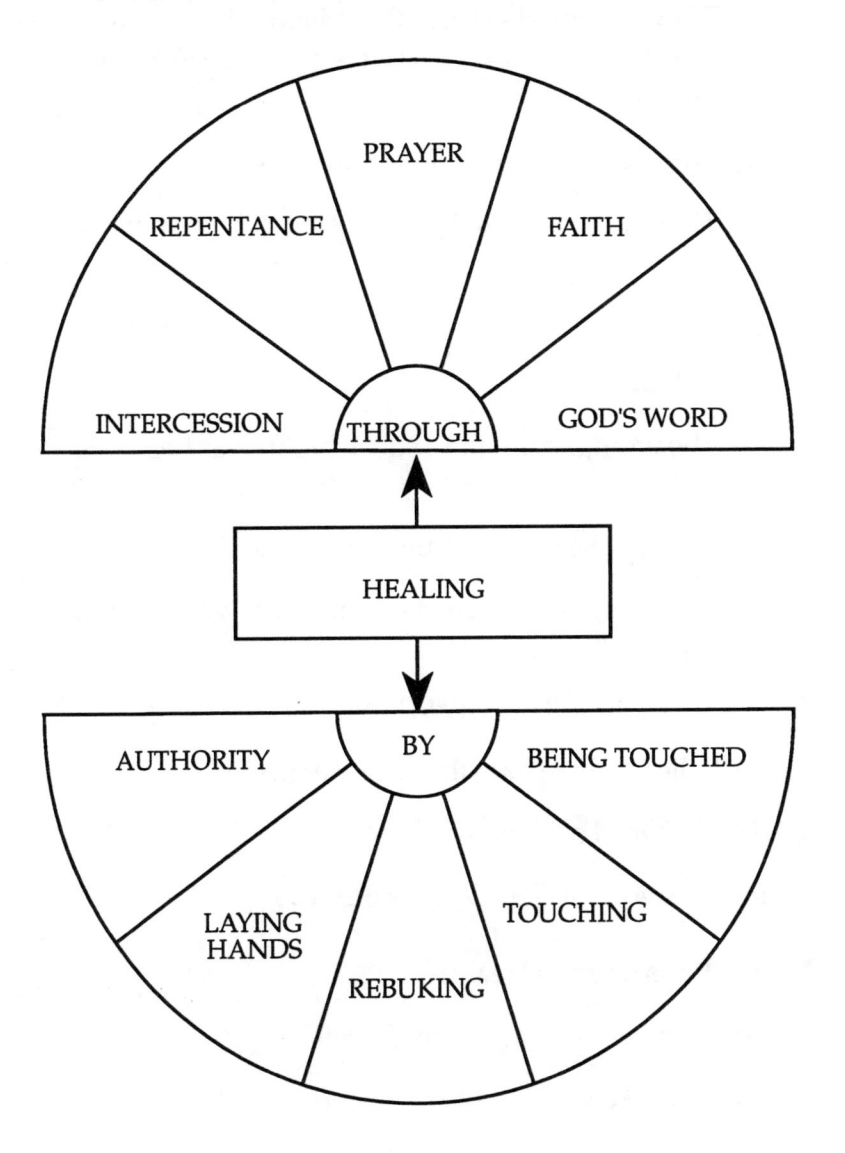

THROUGH:
- PRAYER
- REPENTANCE
- FAITH
- INTERCESSION
- GOD'S WORD

HEALING

BY:
- AUTHORITY
- BEING TOUCHED
- LAYING HANDS
- TOUCHING
- REBUKING

3. Prayer (James 5:14-16)

    (a) The sick should send for the elders of the church to pray over them and anoint them with oil in the name of the Lord.

    (b) The prayer of faith will save the sick.

    (c) The effective, fervent prayer of the righteous man avails much.

    (d) Forgiveness is necessary before healing takes place.

4. Faith (Matt. 9:20-22)

    (a) The woman with the issue of blood was healed by her faith.

    (b) Jesus spoke the word and she was healed.

    (c) The woman touched His hem - faith without works is dead.

5. The word of God (Ps. 119:9,25)

    (a) Believers can claim the promises of God.

    (b) The word of God revives.

    (c) The word of God cleanses our way.

B. Methods Used In Healing

1. Speak the word of authority (Luke 7:1-10)

    (a) Jesus healed the centurion's servant in this way.

    (b) We have the authority in the name of Jesus (John 16:23).

2. The laying on of hands (Mark 5:21-23)

    (a) Jairus came and asked Jesus to lay hands on his daughter who was sick. He went, but was delayed and had to raise her from the dead instead.

    (b) Jesus laid hands on a few sick and healed them (Mark 6:5).

3. Rebuking the sickness (Matt. 8:14)

    (a) Jesus rebuked the fever in Peter's mother-in-law.

4. Touching the Healer (Mark 5:25-29)

    (a) The woman with the issue of blood touched Jesus and was healed.

5. Being touched by the Healer (Matt. 8:3)

    (a) Jesus touched the leper and said, "be cleansed."

V. OBSTACLES TO HEALING (SEE CHART ON NEXT PAGE)

A. The Flow of the Power of the Holy Spirit May Sometimes Be Hindered By:

1. Doubt (James 1:6,7)

    (a) He who doubts is like a wave of the sea, driven and tossed by the wind.

    (b) A doubter receives nothing from the Lord.

2. Sin (Ps. 66:18)

    (a) If we regard iniquity in my heart, the Lord will not hear.

HEALING BLOCKS

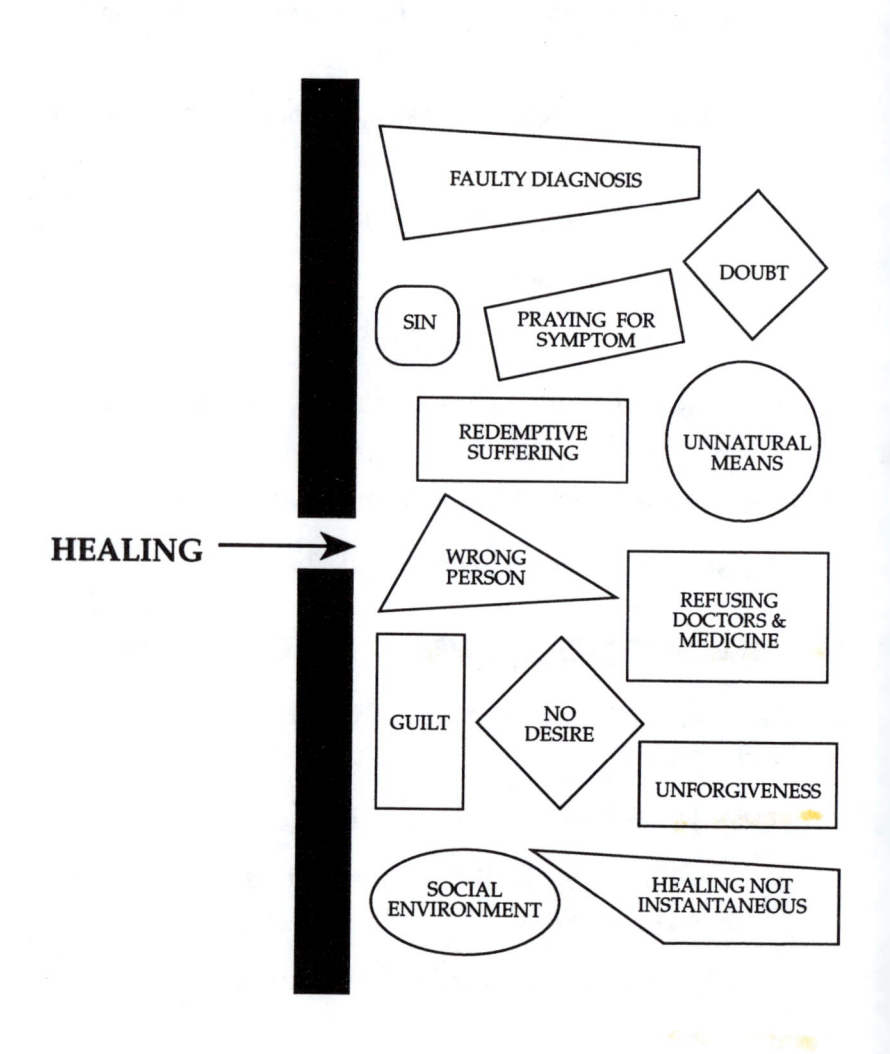

HEALING →

- FAULTY DIAGNOSIS
- DOUBT
- SIN
- PRAYING FOR SYMPTOM
- REDEMPTIVE SUFFERING
- UNNATURAL MEANS
- WRONG PERSON
- REFUSING DOCTORS & MEDICINE
- GUILT
- NO DESIRE
- UNFORGIVENESS
- SOCIAL ENVIRONMENT
- HEALING NOT INSTANTANEOUS

3. No desire to be healed (James 4:2)

    (a) Often we do not have because we do not ask.

4. Redemptive suffering - believing you are suffering for the sake of the kingdom of God.

5. Faulty diagnosis - praying for physical healing when inner healing is required.

    (a) The counselor must be Spirit led.

6. Not praying specifically - the root cause must be discovered.

    (a) It does not profit to pray for a tummy ache, when the ulcer is the root cause.

7. Refusal to see doctors or medicine as one of God's avenues to heal.

8. Not using natural means of preserving health:

    (a) If worries cause headaches, stop worrying.

9. Expecting only instantaneous healing.

    (a) Some are delayed

    (b) Some are gradual

    (c) Others do not occur on the physical level.

10. A different person may be the instrument of healing. We may not have a ministry in that area.

11. The social environment may prevent healing:

    (a) There may be distractions or doubts.

VI. EQUIPPING THE COUNSELOR FOR MINISTRY

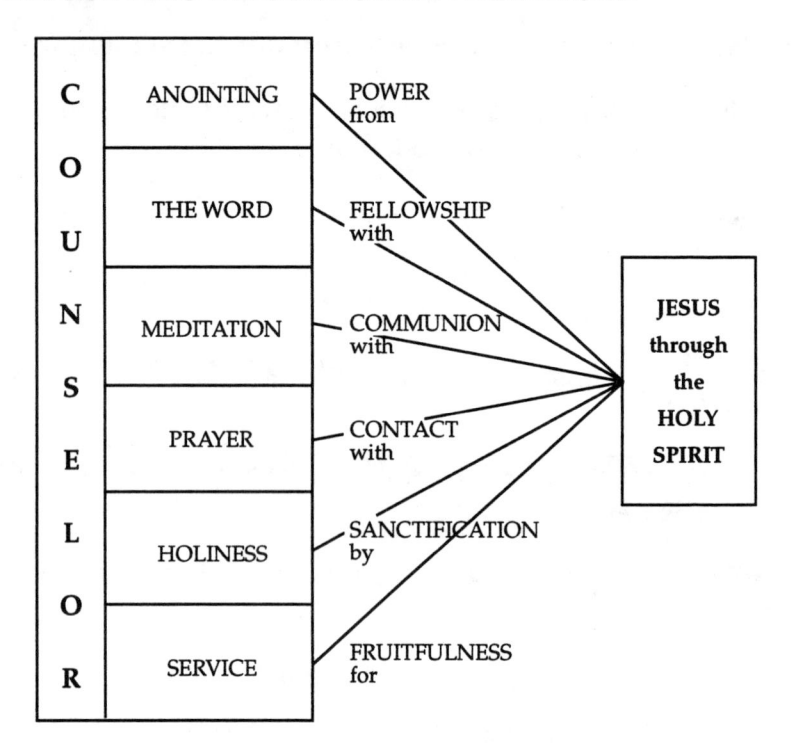

COUNSELOR			
	ANOINTING	POWER from	
	THE WORD	FELLOWSHIP with	JESUS through the HOLY SPIRIT
	MEDITATION	COMMUNION with	
	PRAYER	CONTACT with	
	HOLINESS	SANCTIFICATION by	
	SERVICE	FRUITFULNESS for	

A. The Anointing

1. The counselor must be born again.

2. He needs the pentecostal power of the Holy Spirit (Acts 1:8).

3. We must seek the anointing daily. Oil evaporates, leaks out, loses thickness or viscosity.

B. The Word of God

1. The Word enables us to fellowship with Jesus through His Holy Spirit.

2. God's word heals (Ps. 107:20).

C. Meditation

1. It is through meditation that we have communion with Jesus through His Holy Spirit.

2. Meditating brings understanding (Ps. 119:99).

D. Prayer

1. Prayer allows us contact with Jesus through the Holy Spirit.

2. The effective, fervent prayer of the righteous avails much (James 5:16).

3. The counselor must live a life of prayer - praying earnestly without ceasing.

E. Holiness

1. Holiness is sanctification by Jesus through the Holy Spirit.

2. We are instructed to be holy because God is holy (1 Pet. 1:16).

3. God wants to use clean vessels.

F. Service

1. Service is fruitfulness for Jesus through His Holy Spirit.

2. God equips the saints for service.

3. We are to serve with fervent spirit and diligence (Rom. 12:11).

VII. SOME HELPFUL HINTS FOR HEALING

1. Find out if the person is saved.

2. Heal in Jesus' name.
3. Exercise your faith: "Take up your bed and walk."
4. Let them share their healing - say thanks to God
5. Be moved by love and compassion.
6. Remember that the person prayed for need not be present.
7. Be led by the Holy Spirit.
8. Don't do a deliverance with children, non-believers, or weak Christians around.
9. Speak to the cause rather than the symptom.
10. The power of the Lord must be present.
11. Be bold.
12. Don't advise anyone to come off doctor's medication.
13. Concentrate on one problem at a time.
14. Remember that not all healings are instantaneous or physical. Some take time; some are inner and spiritual.

VIII. PRACTICAL

A. Call for those with physical illnesses in the group and invite them to come forward for healing.

B. Let the others divide into teams of four to six and minister healing to those who came forward.

C. Share what happened in the groups.

LESSON 8

INNER HEALING

I. DEFINITION OF INNER HEALING (SEE CHART ON NEXT PAGE)

A. Deliverance From Bondage (Luke 4:18):

- Healing the broken-hearted

- Deliverance to the captives

- Liberty to the oppressed

B.   Bringing Jesus In Our Lives and Letting Go Hurts

Rita Bennett puts it this way: *"Teaching people to accept the presence of Jesus in their past, present, or future - helping them to forgive everyone and setting them free to live in the present at their fullest potential."*

C.   Releasing the Flow of the Holy Spirit (Rom. 8:2)

Dennis Bennett puts it this way: *"Inner healing is simply cooperating with the Lord to let Him cure and remove from our psychological natures the things that are blocking the flow of the Holy Spirit."*

D. The Bondage is in the Soul (Review "Necessity For The New Birth" chart in Lesson 2)

1. The soul: "psyche" (Greek) - our psychological nature, our feelings, thoughts, drives, desires - the MIND.

> ## WHAT IS INNER HEALING?
>
> "Healing the broken-hearted ...
>
> deliverance to the captives...
>
> liberty to the oppressed..." (Luke 4:18).
>
> "Teaching people to accept the presence of Jesus in their past, present and future - helping them to forgive everyone and setting them free to live in the present at their fullest potential."
>
> *(Rita Bennett)*
>
> "Inner healing is simply cooperating with the Lord to let Him cure and remove from our psychological natures the things that are blocking the flow of the Holy Spirit."
>
> *(Dennis Bennett)*

2. The soul struggles against God (Rom. 7:19).

    "For the good that I will to do, I do not do; but the evil I will not to do, that I practice."

3. The soul is in control before salvation. The spirit must be in control.

4. The soul needs healing.

II. HOW MEMORIES GET STORED

Psychologists through research and observation have written about many of the areas that have affected the psychological well-being of the individual. Many of these have been confirmed through the practical experience of the Christian counselor.

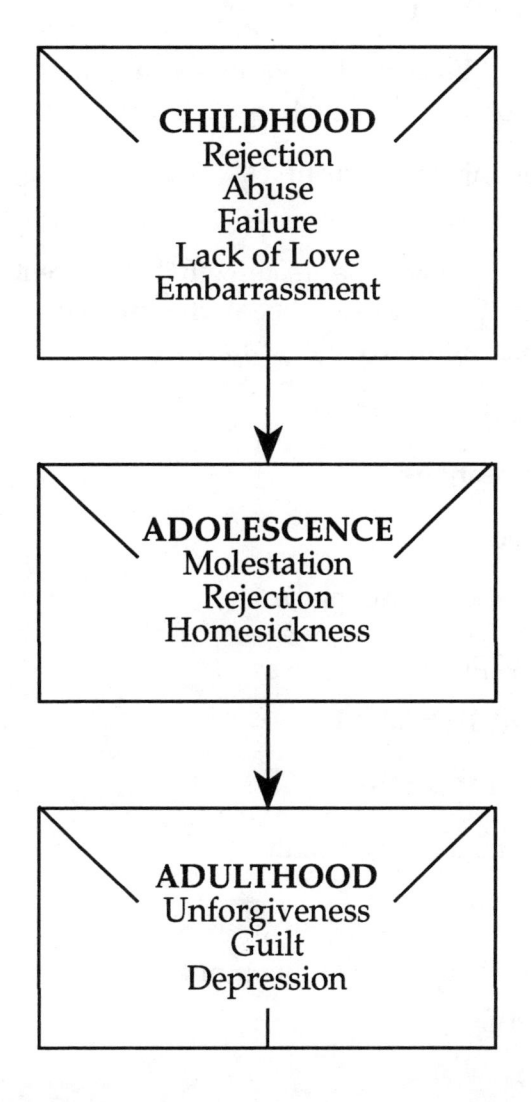

CHILDHOOD
Rejection
Abuse
Failure
Lack of Love
Embarrassment

↓

ADOLESCENCE
Molestation
Rejection
Homesickness

↓

ADULTHOOD
Unforgiveness
Guilt
Depression

A. Childhood Experiences

1. The foundation for our lives is laid in the first five or six years of life.

2. We respond today according to how we were treated as children, and according to the attitudes and opinions instilled in us by our parents.

3. Childhood hurts go deeper than adult hurts because the child is not able to defend himself, fight back, or walk away.

4. Children injured in the first six years need a lot of prayer help.

5. A child needs love - the greatest gift that a parent can give to the child. When this is absent, the little child inside has never been allowed to grow up.

6. Some childhood hurts are:

    - severe beatings

    - rejection

    - being locked in a cupboard

    - death of parent

    - being tied to a table leg

    - divorce of parents

    - being embarrassed openly

    - abuse

    - having a tape put on his mouth to prevent him from speaking.

B. Some Adolescent Experiences

1. At this stage, privacy is important to the adolescent. Violation of this privacy brings hurt.

2. Molestation is common and serious.

3. Rejection by a first love is taken more seriously by the adolescent than some adults realize.

4. Many of these young people are sent off to boarding schools at far too early an age. They miss that parental care, guidance, and relationship.

C. Some Adult Experiences

1. Divorce is traumatic, it is hated by God, and brings separation.

2. Abortion is sin and brings death.

3. An alcoholic mate is a great spiritual test.

4. Adoption, if not handled properly, can create a lot of bitterness and anger.

5. The death of a loved one who is not released brings bondage.

6. Many adults hold anger against God for unfavorable situations in their lives.

7. Abuse, such as rape, is not easy to deal with psychologically.

III. MINISTERING INNER HEALING

DETECTING THE NEED FOR INNER HEALING

1. Acting as a child even in adulthood
2. Compulsive over-eating
3. Wishing to be dead or someone else
4. Unreasonable fears
5. Feeling that everyone is against you
6. Having a physical illness with no known cause
7. Unusually critical of others
8. Falling into frequent depression
9. Having constant nightmares and recurring dreams
10. Holding resentment in your heart for others.

A. Detecting the Need For Inner Healing

When a person is deprived of his childhood activities, a number of behavioral problems are evident in the individual. Discuss the list overpage.

God does not want this for us. In 1 Corinthians 13:11 it says, "When I was a child, I spoke as a child, I understood as a child, I thought as a child; but when I became a man, I put away childish things."

IV. METHODS OF INNER HEALING

A. The Word of God

1. God's Word healed Jeremiah of the insecurity he felt when he was called to God's service:

   "Ah, Lord God, behold I cannot speak, for I am a youth."

   God comforted him: "Do not say 'I am a youth', for you shall go to all to whom I send you, and whatever I command you, you shall speak. Do not be afraid of their faces, for I am with you to deliver you" (Jer. 1:6-8).

2. God's Word healed Elijah from depression:

   When Elijah ran away from the threats of Jezebel, God provided sleep, food, conversation, and ventilation of feeling for him, then changed his perspective by a "still small voice."

B. Through the Anointing That Comes From Praise and Worship

C. Through Deliverance From Evil Spirits

D. Through Praying For Your Enemies In a Positive Way That God Would Let His Perfect Will Be Done In Their Lives

E. Through Inner Healing Prayers - Forgiving, Releasing and Renouncing

Remember, understanding is the key. Ask questions to get helpful information:

When did this all begin?

Who is the first person who ever loved you?

My father made me feel like....

Can you remember a very happy time you had with your mother?

V. INNER HEALING METHODS

A. Asking Jesus to Heal the Memories

1. Ask the counselee to describe the hurtful event as clearly as possible.

2. Let him tell Jesus his feeling, not holding back his emotions.

3. Lead him to forgive in Jesus' name.

4. Jesus is the Healer and He will heal the way he feels about the other person as he talks to Him. Romans 12:2 says "be transformed by the renewing of your minds." Jesus does not blot out memory, He changes attitude.

B. Seeing the Person As Christ Sees Him

1. God calls those things which do not exist as though they did (Rom. 4:17b).

    (a) The counselee must see the enemy as Christ sees him. God made him, loves him, and has given him every chance to be redeemed. Let him imagine what might have caused him to be like that.

    (b) Forgive him.

VI. THE IMPORTANCE OF FORGIVENESS IN INNER HEALING

A. Jesus Commanded Us to Forgive (Matt. 5:24)

1. We must first be willing to forgive.

2. There is no soul healing without the decision to forgive.

B. Forgiving at a Deeper Level

1. Let counselee ask Jesus to help him to want to forgive and speak to the person through Jesus: "I release you in Jesus' name and no longer hold anything against you."

   "I set you free. I set myself free."

   "Jesus has healed me."

2. If the person is dead, ask Jesus to tell him.

3. When you do not forgive your enemy, you are to some extent controlled by him.

4. God cannot protect us from the enemy unless we forgive. When we forgive, we take away the enemy's weapon and make it possible for God to protect us.

5. You know you have forgiven when you can treat the person just as kindly as someone else.

6. Genuine forgiveness manifests itself in love.

7. Tell God when you are angry at Him and forgive Him.

VII. QUALIFICATIONS OF THE COUNSELOR FOR INNER HEALING

A. Requirements of the Counselor *(Discuss)*

1. Must be a born-again believer and a practicing Christian whose life is a good example to others.

2. Must be baptized by the Holy Spirit and is guided by the Holy Spirit during counseling.

3. Must be open to receiving and using the gifts of the Holy Spirit.

4. Must not be in need of inner healing as well, but should be emotionally stable.

5. Must possess a good knowledge of the Word and is able to pray.

6. Must be able to lead others through salvation, baptism of the Holy Spirit, and renouncing cults and occult.

7. Must minister in love and with compassion.

B. Characteristics of the Counselor.

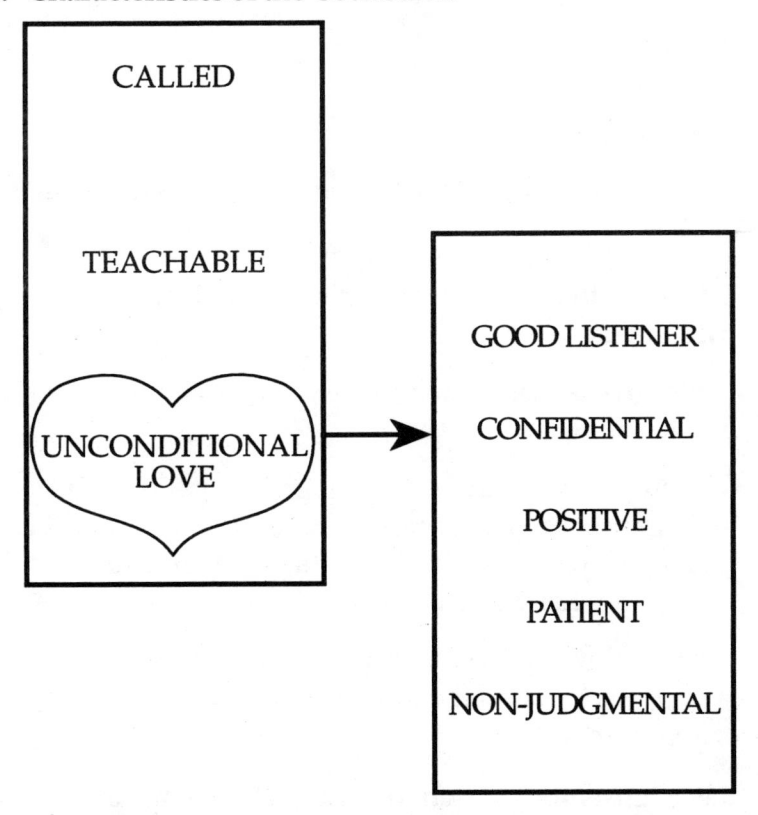

```
┌─────────────────────┐
│      CALLED         │
│                     │   ┌──────────────────┐
│    TEACHABLE        │   │  GOOD LISTENER   │
│                     │   │                  │
│    ╭─────╮          │──▶│  CONFIDENTIAL    │
│   (UNCONDITIONAL)   │   │                  │
│    LOVE             │   │  POSITIVE        │
│    ╰─────╯          │   │                  │
│                     │   │  PATIENT         │
│                     │   │                  │
│                     │   │  NON-JUDGMENTAL  │
└─────────────────────┘   └──────────────────┘
```

1. Loving unconditionally: deep love makes it easier to talk about deep pain. Ask God to baptize you with His love.

2. Non-judgmental: being judgmental deters openness.

3. Confidential

4. Patient: wait for God's direction and for the counselor to start.

5. Being a good listener.

6. Being positive: give hope; God is BIG.

7. Teachability: desire to grow in Christ.
8. Feel called by God.

VIII. PRACTICAL

A. Lead a discussion on the important points covered in this lesson.

B. Minister to counselors to bring inner healing to those who need to be free of:

1. Unforgiveness: let them forgive with the will, then through Jesus.

2. Divorce: work with them through the rejection and guilt they may feel; let them relive the scene; check counselee's relationship with parent of the opposite sex, and heal relationships wherever necessary.

3. Death of loved one: heal guilt, regrets, anger at God. Relive a happy scene, and the funeral, and ask Jesus to help you say good-bye.

C. Let counselors form small groups, choose one inner healing problem from among them, discuss how it is to be dealt with, then do the inner healing.

LESSON 9

ABUSE

I. UNDERSTANDING ABUSE

A. Definition of Abuse

Indulgence in a habit over which we can exercise no control. To use wrongly or misuse. To treat in a harmful or injurious way.

B. Some Types of Abuse:

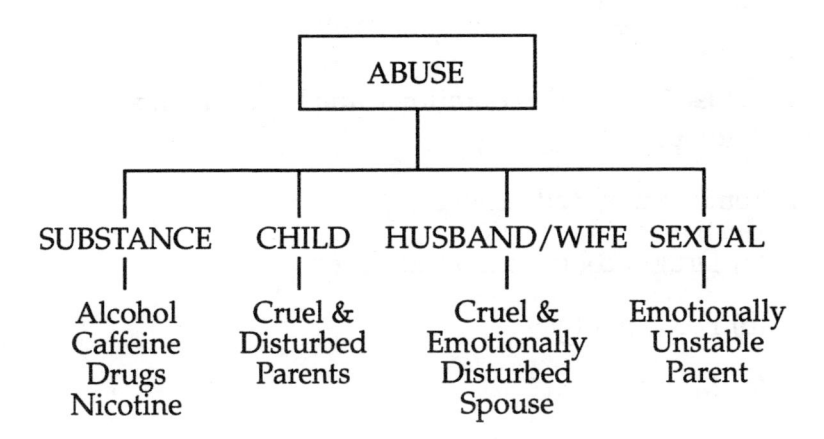

```
                        ABUSE
         ┌──────────┬───────────┬──────────┐
     SUBSTANCE    CHILD    HUSBAND/WIFE  SEXUAL
      Alcohol    Cruel &     Cruel &    Emotionally
      Caffeine  Disturbed  Emotionally   Unstable
      Drugs     Parents    Disturbed     Parent
      Nicotine               Spouse
```

1. Substance abuse - over-indulgence in:

    (a) Alcohol

    (b) Caffeine

(c) Drugs

(d) Nicotine

2. Child abuse - misuse of authority by:

   (a) Cruel and disturbed parents or older siblings

3. Husband/wife abuse - a violation of God's law concerning marital relationships, by:

   (a) Cruel and emotionally disturbed spouse.

4. Sexual abuse - Misuse of a sacred gift of God to husbands and wives by:

   (a) Emotionally unstable people.

Abuse manifests itself in many other ways, but this lesson will deal specifically with substance abuse, child abuse, husband/wife abuse, and sexual abuse.

C. Abuse Can Lead to Emotional and Psychological Addiction

1. Some resulting addictions

   (a) Drug, alcohol, or food addiction

   (b) Pornography

   (c) Masturbation

   (d) Unnatural sex

   (e) Wife-beating

II. SOME TYPES OF ABUSERS

A. Substance Abusers

1. These are individuals who are not able to control their desires for alcohol, drugs, nicotine, food, caffeine, and other substances, and indulge in the habit compulsively.

2. As a result their personality traits are intensified:

    (a) One with a tendency to be rebellious becomes more rebellious.

    (b) Jealousy is intensified and may result in hate.

    (c) Anger becomes wrath.

3. They overcompensate in everything to cover up for inadequacies:

    (a) The giver becomes over-generous.

    (b) The daring becomes dangerously risky.

    (c) The humble gives up his own rights unnecessarily.

4. All areas of the abusers' lives are affected by the abuse:

    (a) Home

    (b) Work

    (c) Community

B. Child Abusers

1. These are parents who become abnormally angry and overreact, hurting the child cruelly, and injuring him physically, morally, or mentally.

2. They are very demanding, wanting to be obeyed promptly and without questions.

3. They use cruelty and punishment rather than reasonable and loving discipline.

4. They were probably abused as children themselves.

C. Husband/Wife Abusers

1. They "put down" the spouse by abusive language and threats which are destructive to the spouse's personality. Physical abuse often follows.

2. They have low self-esteem and usually consider themselves failures.

3. They relate poorly to people and have insatiable egos.

4. They are jealous and often accuse mate of unfaithfulness.

5. They tend to control all of spouse's activities.

6. They never accept blame for failure, and never admit guilt.

7. They often beat their spouse.

8. Alcohol or drug abuse and childhood hurts are sometimes causes.

D. Sexual Abusers

1. They may be men or women who are emotionally loners, although they do not manifest this in appearance.

2. They have a quiet interest in their daughter's or son's activities, and become more and more domineering regarding their children's actions.

3. They are feelingless and self-centered people, who have deliberately shut out the world around them.
4. They will not allow themselves to develop relationships with others, and they see people as things to be used.
5. Abuse to them has become a way of life, and they have developed mechanisms to defend themselves against those who would break in on their little world. They threaten, coerce, and intimidate.
6. They have become almost chronic liars, and will not admit to their habit. They should not be trusted.
7. Many abusers were also abused as children.

III. COUNSELING THE ABUSER

1. Speak in love.
2. Recognize the problem as sin.
3. Give hope through the Scriptures (1 John 1:9).
4. Lead him to Christ.
5. Help counselee choose to do right.
6. Advise counselee to participate in Bible studies and prayer groups.
7. Help him to adopt a new style of life.
8. Bring healing to the root of the problem.
9. Pray with the counselee.
10. Give counselee support with Scriptural references.
11. Refer counselee where necessary.

A. See the Abuser As Someone Who Is Also In Need of Spiritual Help.

1. Talk to him in love.

2. Help him to recognize that his problem is sin, but do not be judgmental.

3. Tell him that there is hope for him through the Scriptures, because Jesus has come to set the captives free (Luke 4:18).

4. Inquire of him whether he has ever had a personal relationship with Jesus Christ, and if necessary, share the Gospel with him, leading him to salvation (1 John 1:9).

5. Help him to see that it is easier to break a bad habit by letting Jesus put a good habit in its place. Share the fruit of the spirit with him (Gal. 5:22,23).

6. Suggest to him a good Bible study group and a church that teaches the Word of God.

7. In case of drug or alcohol addiction, Paul's words in 2 Cor. 6:17 may have to be applied:

    "Come out from among them, and be separate...."

    They should forsake old circle of friends, and avoid activities related to the habit they are trying to break. The alcoholic needs to adopt a lifestyle of total abstinence.

8. Try to determine the root cause of the abuse problem e.g.:

    - the need to be loved

    - the need to feel important

    - the need for security.

9. Pray with the counselee for healing for those areas, e.g.: unforgiveness, rejection.

10. Give him support with these scriptural references:

    Matt. 11:28 1; Pet. 5:7; Prov. 3:56; Ps. 34:4,5; Is. 26:3,4, 11.

    Refer both the abuser and the abused when necessary:

    Abusive parents - to some Christian psychologist or family counseling center

    Alcoholic - to Alcoholic Anonymous

    Drug addict - to a drug rehabilitation center.

IV. COUNSELING THE ABUSED

1. Encourage the counselee to talk.
2. Inform him that he need not be the victim anymore. He has legal rights.
3. Encourage him to break the cycle of abuse by receiving counseling.
4. Assure him of God's love and show him how Jesus, too, was abused.
5. Pray with him for strength and understanding (Matt. 11:28).
6. Ensure he has salvation.
7. Encourage him to join a church.
8. Encourage participation in Bible studies and prayer groups.

9. Help him to forgive.
10. Help him discover his identity in Christ.
11. Help him to accept responsibility for his response to being abused.

A. See the Abused As Victims

1. Deal with the individual with love, understanding, and patience.

2. The victim may never have expressed himself or herself:

    (a) Encourage him or her to talk.

3. The abused has probably been blamed for everything:

    (a) Inform him that he need not be a victim anymore. Jesus can set him free (Luke 4:18).

4. The person has been the victim of a cycle of abuse:

    (a) Encourage him to break the cycle of abuse by receiving counseling:

    (b) If necessary refer to a Pastor or family counselor.

    (c) Assure him of God's love and how Jesus, too, was abused.

5. Many of them feel unloved, discouraged and wished they were dead:

    (a) Pray with them for strength and understanding (Matt. 11:28).

    (b) Explain to them the love of the cross of Christ.

6. The victim may not know Jesus personally, or may have backslidden:

- (a) Ensure that he has salvation.
- (b) Present the Gospel to him if necessary.

7. He may not be a part of a church, or the church had not helped his situation:

    (a) Encourage him to join a good Bible-teaching church.

8. The abused needs the word of God:

    (a) Encourage him to participate in a Bible study and prayer group.

9. The victim has been deeply hurt:

    (a) Help him to forgive.

10. He has probably lost his identity:

    (a) Help him to discover who he is in Christ

    (i) A new creation (1 Cor. 5:17)

    (ii) A free person (John 8:36).

11. The victim has developed low self-esteem:

    (a) Help him to accept responsibility for his response to being abused.

V. PRACTICAL

A. **Ask for a volunteer to share an abuse problem with the group. Do a case study of this problem.**

B. **Divide the group into prayer partners and allow them to pray for each other's needs in the area of abuse. If there are no such needs, they should pray for similar needs of others.**

NOTES

LESSON 10

DEMON DELIVERANCE

I. DEFINITION OF DELIVERANCE

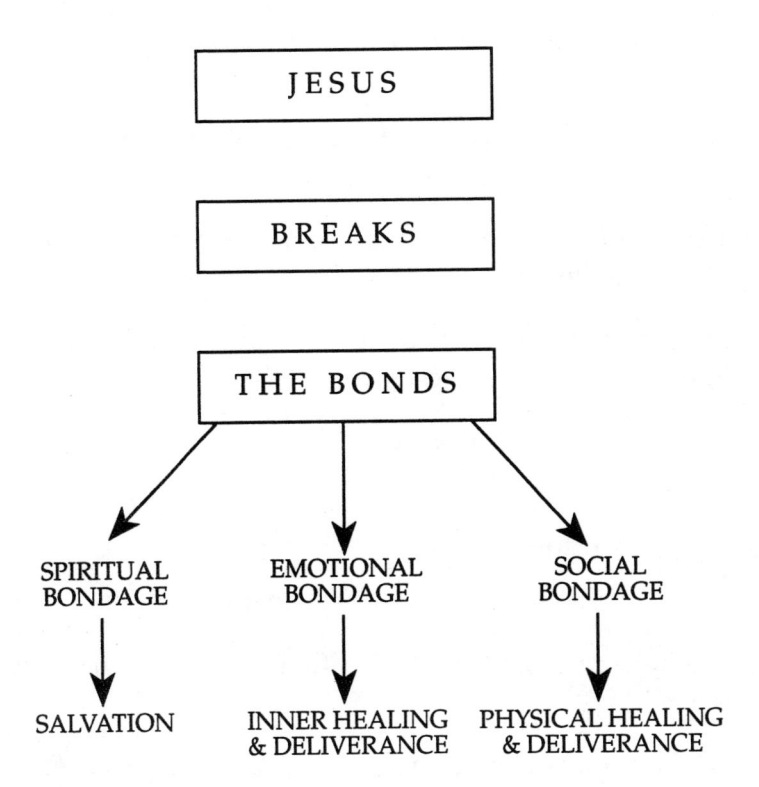

```
          JESUS

         BREAKS

        THE BONDS
       /    |    \
      ↓     ↓     ↓
 SPIRITUAL EMOTIONAL SOCIAL
 BONDAGE   BONDAGE   BONDAGE
    ↓         ↓         ↓
 SALVATION INNER HEALING PHYSICAL HEALING
           & DELIVERANCE & DELIVERANCE
```

A. Being Set Free From Bondage

1. Jesus Christ is the Deliverer (Rom. 10:13).

2. He sets us free from physical, emotional, social, and spiritual bondage (John 8:32,36).

3. There is a close relationship between deliverance and healing which follows deliverance.

II. SPIRITUAL BONDAGE

A. Demons

1. Demons are disembodied evil spirits that can invade and indwell the human body.

2. Each demon is a specialist, identified by his nature, e.g., rebellion.

3. They are most often found in colonies or families headed by a domineering man.

4. The domineering man must be commanded out with his family in the name of Jesus, e.g.:

Domineering man: depression

Family:	- despair	- despondency
	- suicide	- dejection
	- discouragement	- death

5. Demons cannot possess Christians, but they can oppress them.

   (a) Christians were bought by the blood of Jesus (1 Pet. 1:18,19).

(b) The body of the believer is the temple of the Holy Spirit (1 Cor. 6:19,20), but we can allow it to be oppressed by such things as:
- defeatism   - insomnia

B. Fallen Angels

1. These beings have spiritual bodies and therefore, do not inhabit people or animals.

2. They are the "principalities ... powers ... rulers of the darkness of this age ... spiritual hosts of wickedness in the heavenly places" (Eph. 6:12).

3. They are of the devil's kingdom and are highly organized to carry out wicked assignments over influential people or a body of people, governments, churches, etc.

4. The church, for example, may recognize them in the form of:

   - spirit of strife   - doctrinal spirits
   - ritualism   - denominationalism
   - human talent vs. the power of the Holy Spirit.

5. These must be dealt with in spiritual warfare, using spiritual weapons to break their power from over the believer (Eph. 6:10-12; 2 Cor. 10:3,4).

This lesson, however, is not intended to deal with warfare against fallen angels or spiritual beings in the heavenlies, but with the deliverance of a person from an indwelling demon.

C. How Demons Enter the Human Being

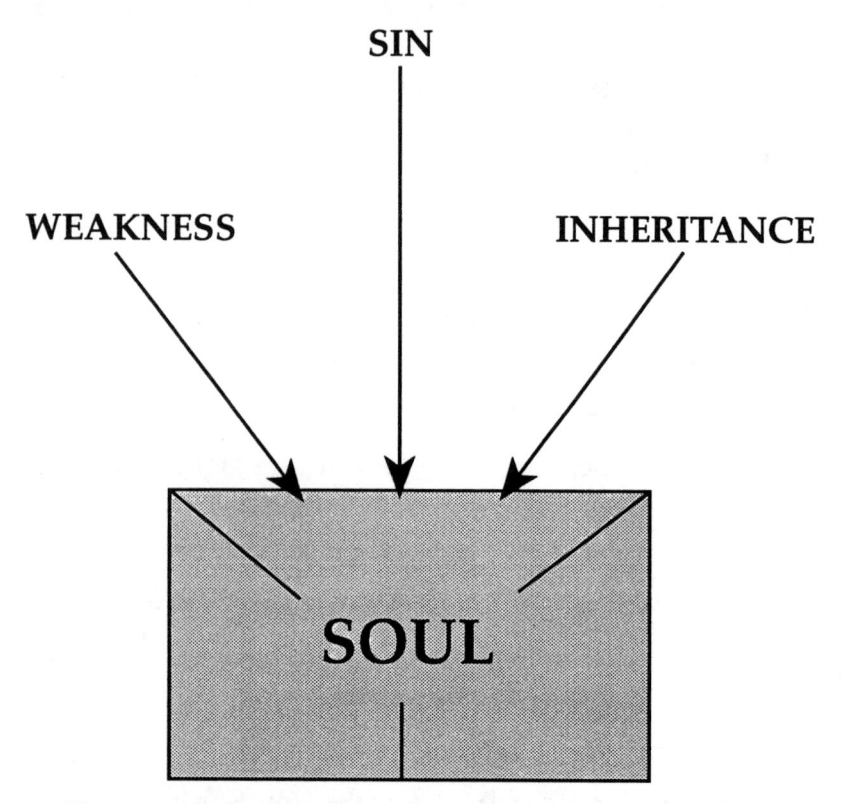

```
         SIN
          │
          ▼
WEAKNESS     INHERITANCE
    ↘    ↓    ↙
    ┌─────────┐
    │  SOUL   │
    └─────────┘
```

1. They enter through open doors when we commit sins of omission or commission, e.g.:

    - failure to forgive   - sin of omission

    - works of the flesh   - sins of commission (Gal. 5:19-21).

2. Doors are opened in times of weakness, e.g.:

    - childhood   - depression

3. They enter through inheritance. We accept the lies and fears suggested by the devil, that we inherit these things from our parents, e.g.:

   - mental illness   - early death

God will choose our inheritance for us (Ps. 47:4).

C. The Christian's Responsibility

1. Demons must also be dealt with in spiritual warfare (Eph. 6:10-12)

2. Spiritual weapons must be used (2 Cor. 10:3,4).

3. Demons must be cast out in the name of Jesus (Mark 16:17).

4. The believer receives power after the Holy Ghost has come upon him (Acts 1:8).

5. The counselor should ask God for the gifts of discerning of spirits and the word of knowledge. These gifts are indispensable to spiritual warfare.

III. THE IMPORTANCE OF DELIVERANCE

A. Demons are Enemies of the Gifts and Fruit of the Spirit (See chart on next page):

1. They keep the gifts from coming forth in the Christian's life, and hinder his preparation for the Lord's coming e.g.

   The spirit of doubt may hinder prophecy.

   "let us prophesy in proportion to our faith..." (Rom. 12:6b).

   The spirit of resentment and rejection may hinder love.

WHY DELIVERANCE?

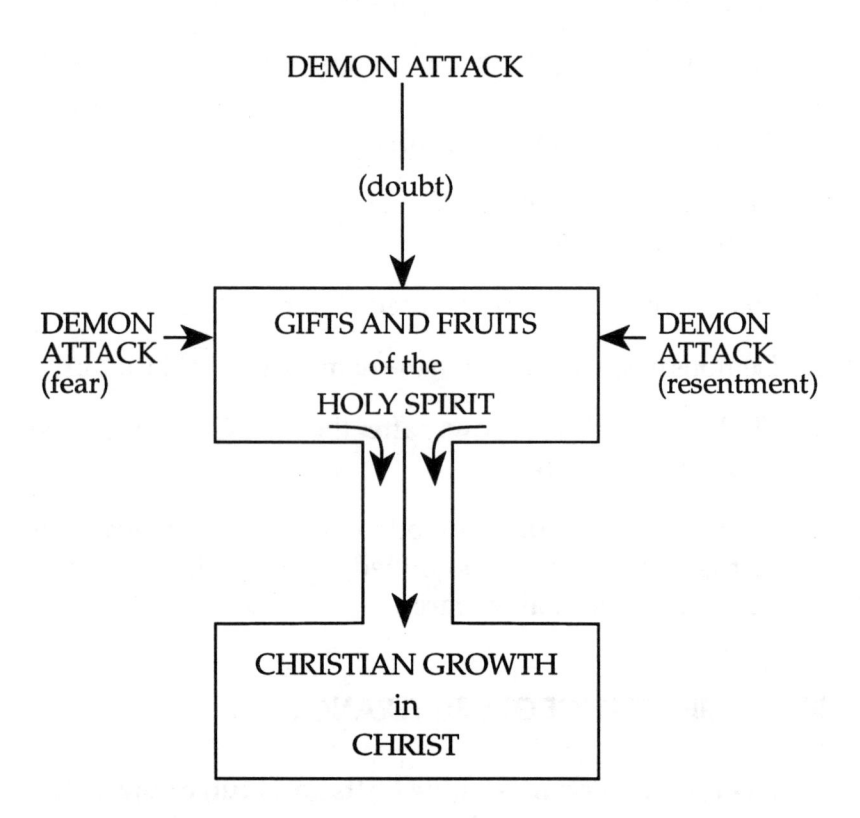

```
                    DEMON ATTACK
                         |
                      (doubt)
                         ↓
  DEMON   →     ┌─────────────────┐    ←   DEMON
  ATTACK        │ GIFTS AND FRUITS │        ATTACK
  (fear)        │     of the      │        (resentment)
                │   HOLY SPIRIT   │
                └────────┬────────┘
                         ↓
                ┌─────────────────┐
                │ CHRISTIAN GROWTH│
                │       in        │
                │     CHRIST      │
                └─────────────────┘
```

IV. DETERMINING THE NEED FOR DELIVERANCE

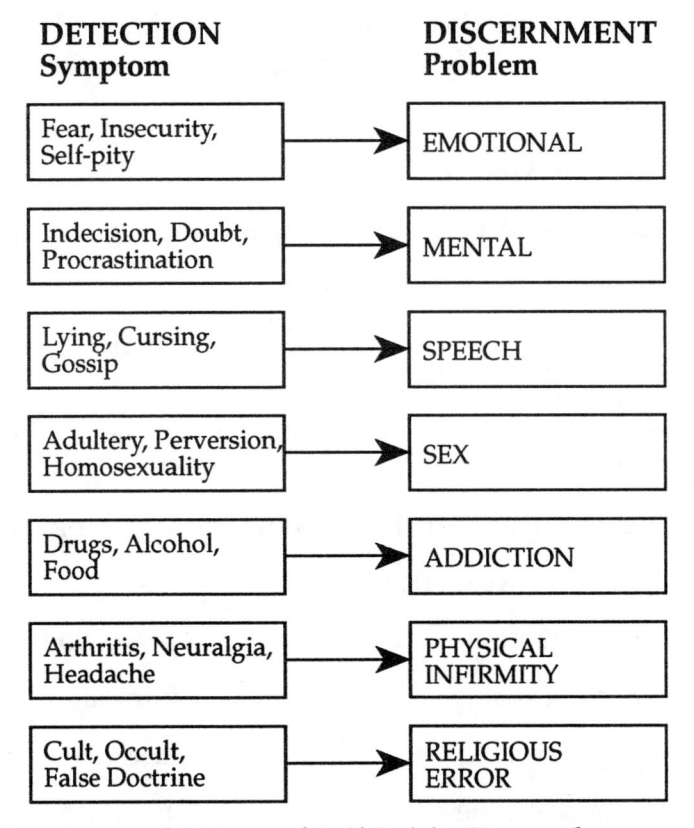

DETECTION Symptom	DISCERNMENT Problem
Fear, Insecurity, Self-pity	EMOTIONAL
Indecision, Doubt, Procrastination	MENTAL
Lying, Cursing, Gossip	SPEECH
Adultery, Perversion, Homosexuality	SEX
Drugs, Alcohol, Food	ADDICTION
Arthritis, Neuralgia, Headache	PHYSICAL INFIRMITY
Cult, Occult, False Doctrine	RELIGIOUS ERROR

A. Presence and Nature of Evil Spirits Known by:

1. Discernment (1 Cor. 12:11) - a gift of the Holy Spirit.

2. Detection - observing what the spirits are doing in the person.

B. Detection of Demons:

1. Emotional problems:

    (a) Persistent emotional disturbances - hatred, self-pity, fear, rejection, insecurity.

2. Mental problems:

    (a) Disturbances in the mind or thought life - indecision, doubt, compromise, confusion, procrastination, rationalization.

3. Speech problems:

    (a) Outbursts of uncontrollable use of the tongue

    - lying
    - blasphemy
    - mockery
    - cursing
    - criticism
    - gossip
    - railing

4. Sex problems:

    (a) Recurring unclean thoughts and acts regarding sex:

    - fantasy sex experiences
    - lust
    - masturbation
    - perversions
    - homosexuality
    - fornication
    - adultery
    - incest
    - provocativeness
    - harlotry

5. Addictions:

    (a) Being controlled by a habit:

    - nicotine
    - alcohol
    - drugs
    - medicine
    - caffeine
    - food

6. Physical infirmities:

    (a) The demon of infirmity inflicts us with a disease

e.g., the woman inflicted with an infirmity for eighteen years (Luke 13:11).

(b) When the demon of infirmity is cast out, pray for healing of whatever damage has resulted.

7. Religious Error:

(a) Involvement to any degree in religious error, by personal contact or literature:

   (i) False religions: Eastern religions, mind sciences, yoga, karate which cannot be divorced from heathen worship.

   (ii) Cults: Mormonism, Jehovah's Witnesses, Christian Science, bloodless religions which deny the power of the blood of Jesus. These have a form of godliness, but deny power (2 Tim. 3:5).

   (iii) Occult: seances, ouji boards, witchcraft, horoscopes, palmistry, hypnosis, extra-sensory perception. Any supernatural knowledge, wisdom, guidance and power apart from God is forbidden (Deut. 18:9-15).

   (iv) False doctrine: promoted by seducing spirits in the last days (1 Tim. 4:1). The doctrine is designed to attack the deity and humanity of Jesus Christ, to deny the inspiration of the scriptures, to distract Christians from the move of the spirit, to cause disunity in the body of Christ, to cause confusion in the Church, to puff people up to become unteachable, and to foster fleshly activities as the gateway to the spiritual e.g. asceticism, vegetarianism.

V. DEMON MANIFESTATIONS

A. The Nature of Demons

When demons are confronted and pressured through spiritual warfare, including a praise environment, they sometimes demonstrate their particular natures through the person in a variety of ways:

1. As a serpent:
   - sticking out the tongue
   - pushing the tongue in and out rapidly
   - hissing through the nose
   - writhing over the floor
   - eyes characteristic of a snake's eyes.

2. In the hands:
   - hands numb and tingle
   - fingers extended and rigid

   (a) May indicate arthritic spirit, lust, suicide, murder, or others associated with wrong use of the hands.

   (b) The victim should shake hands vigorously to dislodge the spirits.

3. Eyelids are open, eyeballs roll into the head, and skin is waxen:

   (a) This is the death spirit

   (b) The person might have been close to death through serious illness or attempted suicide.

4. Unpleasant odor:

    (a) A smell similar to that of a cancer hospital, or boiled cabbage, comes from the victim.

5. Demons may cry out with loud voices (Matt. 8:29):

    (a) They sometimes use the voice of a child, or use a man's voice in a woman's body.

    (b) They may identify themselves.

    (c) They claim right to their "house" - the individual's body.

    (d) They pretend to be gone.

6. A haughty look:

    (a) A spirit of pride may be present.

    (b) This will cause people to think more highly of themselves than they ought.

7. Pantomiming:

    (a) Demon of worldly dancing.

8. Sleeping and yawning:

    (a) Religious spirit.

9. Pain in the back of the neck:

    (a) Nervousness and tension.

10. Laughing:

    (a) Spirit of mockery. When demons are cast out, they normally leave through the mouth or nose, sometimes manifested by coughing, bringing up phlegm, yawning, vomiting, spitting, foaming, or sighing. Rarely does food substance come up from the stomach.

VI. CASTING OUT DEMONS

A. Some Guidelines

There are no "cut and dried" techniques. The important thing is to be open to the Holy Spirit.

1. Let the Holy Spirit lead.
2. Prepare the counselee for deliverance. Talk to him and ensure salvation.
3. Don't converse with the demons unless the Holy Spirit indicates some specific purpose in doing so.
4. Differentiate between demon's and victim's voice.
5. Use deliverance teams of two to six people - both men and women would be wise. A man should not minister alone to a woman or vice versa. The team must be in unity, and may alternate leadership while others pray, read the Scriptures, or sing songs emphasizing the blood of Jesus.
6. Pray a deliverance prayer with the counselee:

    - confessing sins

    - forgiving and asking forgiveness

    - renouncing Satan and all his works

    - claiming redemption by the blood

- calling on the name of Jesus to be saved

- binding Satan and his demons, commanding them to leave, and loosing the victim in the name of Jesus (Matt. 16:18,19). We can bind an evil spirit in someone else, even though he does not know it.

B. Other General Guidelines

1. Deliverance of a non-believer:

    (a) Priority is salvation

    (b) He must want deliverance, and even if he consents and does not have salvation, demons will return.

2. Delivering children:

    (a) Give them simple explanation of what you are doing, and let them know you are not talking to them, but to unruly spirits.

    (b) Speak quietly but with authority.

    (c) Parents have responsibility to protect children from demons.

3. Deliverance may be done in a church service, but the minister must determine if appropriate, e.g., if a person interrupts the preacher.

4. Deliverance may be done on an individual, or with a group. Many helpers are needed with a group ministry. This is effective with children. Demons common to many people are called out, e.g., fear, resentment, anger, selfishness.

5. Deliverance may be public or private. Let the Holy Spirit decide.

6. Experience will increase confidence. The minister is operating in the power and authority granted him.

VII. TO PREVENT THE RETURN OF DEMONS

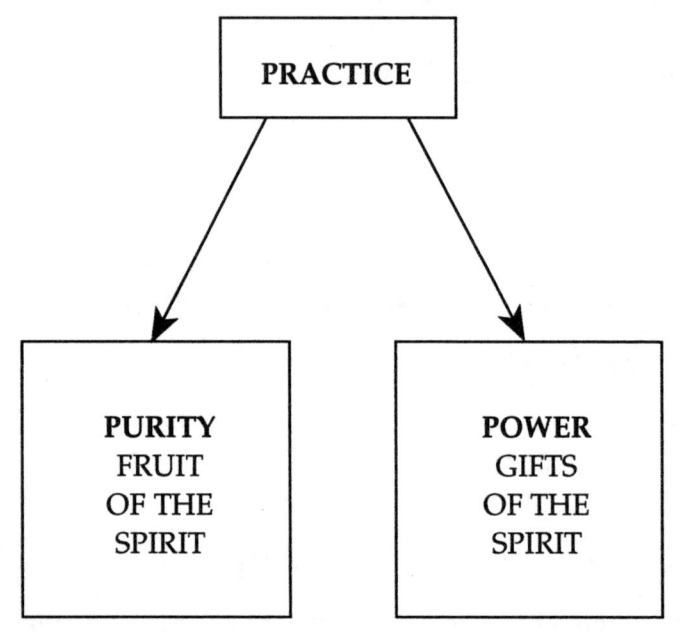

```
            PRACTICE
           /        \
          ↓          ↓
      PURITY       POWER
      FRUIT        GIFTS
      OF THE       OF THE
      SPIRIT       SPIRIT
```

A. Matthew 12:43-45 tells us demons may return if the house is empty.

1. We must fill the house with Jesus:

    (a) Practice purity - the fruit of the Spirit.

    (b) Practice power - the gifts of the Spirit. e.g. The baptism of the Holy Spirit often comes when demons are cast out.

VIII. SELF-DELIVERANCE

A. A Believer Can Deliver Himself From Oppression:

1. Proceed in the same manner as for others, except you are your own minister.

2. Pray the deliverance prayer.

3. The danger is that we often do not see faults in ourselves.

4. Steps to deliverance:

    - honesty: confess

    - humility: depend on God

    - repentance: turn away from sin

    - renunciation: make a clean break from Satan and all his works

    - forgiveness: be willing to forgive and be forgiven

    - prayer: ask God to deliver and set you free (Joel 2:32)

    - warfare: identify, bind and cast out demons in the name of Jesus

IX. A COUNSELOR AS A DELIVERANCE MINISTER

A. Jesus is calling forth laborers into the harvest (Matt. 9:38).

B. We Must Overcome the Fear of Demons and of Men, and Not Permit Satan to Work Unchallenged.

C. Discipleship Has A Cost In Time, Patience, and Energy.

D. **We Must Be Dedicated - Have Compassion, Be Free From Blame, Pray and Fast to Crucify the Flesh, and Bear Each Other's Burdens.**

E. **There Are Benefits:**

1. Rejoicing over liberated souls.

2. Getting to know people quickly, as all pretense is set aside.

3. Experiencing deliverance as the answer to many counseling problems.

4. Spiritual awareness is quickened.

X. PRACTICAL

A. Lead a discussion on important points in the lesson.

B. Ask for someone feeling the need for deliverance, to volunteer to be used to demonstrate deliverance to the class.

C. Minister group deliverance on the following spirits:

- fear	- pride	- religion
- worry	- impatience	- rebellion
- insecurity	- doubt	- rejection

OTHER BOOKS FROM
Pneuma Life Publishing

Water in the Wilderness
by T.D. Jakes
Just before you apprehend your greatest conquest, expect the greatest struggle. Many are perplexed who encounter this season of adversity. This book is designed as a map. (1) It will show you how to survive the worst of times with the greatest of ease; (2) It will cause fountains of living waters to break forth out of the parched, sun drenched areas in your life. This word is literally a stream in the desert. To the weary traveler I say, Come and drink!

Why?
by T.D. Jakes
Why is it that the righteous, who have committed their entire lives to obeying God seem to endure so much pain and experience such conflict? These are perplexing questions that plagued and bewildered Christians as well as unbelievers for ages. In this anointed and inspirational new book, "WHY" Bishop T.D. Jakes, the preacher with the velvet touch and explosive delivery, provocatively and skillfully answers these questions and many more as well as answering the "WHY" of the Anointed.

The Flaming Sword
by Tai Ikomi
Scripture memorization and meditation bring tremendous spiritual power, however many Christians find it to be an uphill task. Committing Scriptures to memory will transform the mediocre Christian to a spiritual giant. This book will help you to become addicted to the powerful practice of scripture memorization and help you obtain the victory that you desire in every area of your life. The Flaming Sword is your pathway to spiritual growth and a more intimate relationship with God.

Opening the Front Door of Your Church
by Dr. Leonard Lovett
A creative approach for small to medium churches who want to develop a more effective ministry. Did you know that 75% of churches in the United States have 150 attendance? Opening the Front Door of your Church is an insightful and creative approach to church development and expansion, especially for churches within the urban environment.

This is My Story
by Candi Staton
This is My Story is a touching Autobiography about a gifted young child who rose from obscurity and poverty to stardom and wealth. With million-selling albums and a top-charting music career, came a life of heart-brokenness, loneliness and despair. This book will make you both cry and laugh as you witness one woman's search for success and love.

Another Look at Sex
by Charles Phillips
This book is undoubtedly a head turner and eye opener that will cause you to take another close look at sex. In this book, Charles Phillips openly addresses this seldom discussed subject and giver life-changing advice on sex to married couples and singles. If you have questions about sex, this is the book for you.

Four Laws of Productivity
by Dr. Mensa Otabil
Success has no favorites. But it does have associates. Success will come to anyone who will pay the price to receive its benefits. *Four Laws of Productivity* will give you four powerful keys that will help you achieve your life's goals. *Four Laws of Productivity* by Dr. Mensa Otabil will show you how to: Discover God's gift in you, develop your gift, perfect your gift, and utilized your gift to its maximum potential. The principles revealed in this timely book will radically change your life.

Single Life
by Earl D. Johnson
The book gives a fresh light on practical issues such as coping with sexual desires, loneliness and preparation for future mate. Written in a lively style, the author admonishes the singles to seek first the Kingdom of God and rest assured in God's promise to supply their needs.... including a life partner!

Strategies for Saving the Next Generation
by Dave Burrows
This book will teach you how to start and effectively operate a vibrant youth ministry. This book is filled with practical tips and insight gained over a number of years working with young people from the street to the parks to the church. Dave Burrows offers the reader vital information that will produce results if carefully considered and adapted. Excellent for Pastors and Youth Pastor as well as youth workers and those involved with youth ministry.

The Church   A Mystery Revealed
by Turnel Nelson
In this book, Pastor Turnel Nelson addresses and outlines some of the fundamental measures that need to be taken in order to revitalize the Church for 21st century evangelism and discipleship.

The Call of God
by Jefferson Edwards
The Call of God will help you to: • Have clarity from God as to what ministry involves • Be able to identify and affirm the call in your life • See what stage you are in your call from God • Remove confusion in relation to the processing of a call or the making of the person • Understand the development of the anointing to fulfill your call.

Come, Let Us Pray
by Emmette Weir
Are you satisfied with your prayer Life? Are you finding that your prayers are often dull, repetitive and lacking in spiritual power? Are you looking for ways to improve your relationship with God? Would you like to be able to pray more effectively? Then *Come, Let Us Pray* will help you in these areas and more. If you want to gain the maximum spiritual experience from your prayer life and enter into the very presence of God. *Come, Let Us Pray.*

Leadership in the New Testament Church
by Earl D. Johnson
Leadership in the New Testament Church offers practical and applicable insight into the role of leadership in the present day church. In this book, the author explains the qualities that leaders must have, explores the interpersonal relationships between the leader and his staff, the leaders' influence in the church and society and how to handle conflicts that arise among leaders.

Becoming A Leader
by Myles Munroe
Becoming A Leader uncovers the secrets of dynamic leadership that will show you how to be a leader in your family, school, community, church and job.
Where ever you are or whatever you do in life this book can help you inevitably become a leader. Remember it is never too late to become a leader. As in every tree there is a forest, so in every follower there is a leader.

Becoming A Leader Workbook
by Myles Munroe
Now you can activate your leadership potential through the **Becoming A Leader Workbook**. This workbook has been designed to take you step by step through the leadership principles taught in Becoming A Leader. As you participate in the work studies in this workbook you will see the true leader inside you develop and grow into maturity. "Knowledge **with action produces results.**"

Mobilizing Human Resources
by Richard Pinder
Pastor Pinder gives an in-depth look at how to organize, motivate and deploy members of the body of Christ in a manner that produces maximum effect for your ministry. This book will assist you in organizing and motivating your 'troops' for effective and efficient ministry. It will also help the individual believer in recognizing their place in the body, using their God given abilities and talents to maximum effect.

The Minister's Topical Bible
by Derwin Stewart
The Minister's Topical Bible covers every aspect of the ministry providing quick and easy access to scriptures in a variety of ministry related topics. This handy reference tool can be effectively used in leadership training, counseling, teaching, sermon preparation and personal study.

The Believer's Topical Bible
by Derwin Stewart
The Believer's Topical Bible covers every aspect of a Christian's relationship with God and man, providing biblical answers and solutions for all challenges. It is a quick, convenient, and thorough reference Bible that has been designed for use in personal devotions, and group bible studies. Over 3500 verses that are systematically organized under 240 topics, and is the largest devotional-topical Bible available in NIV and KJV.

The Layman's Guide to Counseling
by Susan Wallace
The increasing need for counseling has caused today's Christian leaders to become more sensitive to raise up lay-counselors to share this burden with them. Jesus' command is to *"set the captives free."* The Layman's guide to Counseling shows you how.

All books available at your Local Book store or by contacting:

Pneuma Life Publishing
P.O. Box 10612,
Bakersfield, CA 93389-0612

1-800-727-3218
1-805-324-1741